THE WINNING WAY IN GOLF AND LIFE

DR. MORRIS PICKENS

FOREWORD BY ZACH JOHNSON

Thomas Nelson
Since 1798

NASHVILLE   DALLAS   MEXICO CITY   RIO DE JANEIRO

Published in Nashville, Tennessee, by Thomas Nelson.

Cover and interior design by Thinkpen Design.

Photographs by Tim Brown Photography, St. Simons Island, Georgia

Permission to use photographs of TPC Sawgrass given by PGA Tour.

Thomas Nelson titles may be purchased in bulk for educational, business, fund-raising, or sales promotional use. For information, please e-mail SpecialMarkets@ThomasNelson.com.

Unless otherwise indicated, Scripture quotations are taken from the Holy Bible, NEW INTERNATIONAL VERSION®, NIV®. Copyright © 1973, 1978, 1984, 2011 by Biblica, Inc.™ Used by permission. All rights reserved worldwide. Scriptures marked NKJV are taken from THE NEW KING JAMES VERSION.® © 1982 by Thomas Nelson. Used by permission. All rights reserved. Scripture quotations marked MSG are taken from The Message by Eugene H. Peterson. © 1993, 1994, 1995, 1996, 2000, 2001, 2002. Used by permission of NavPress Publishing Group. All rights reserved. Scripture quotations marked TLB are taken from The Living Bible. © 1971. Used by permission of Tyndale House Publishers, Inc., Wheaton, Illinois 60189. All rights reserved.

ISBN-13: 978-14003-2406-4

Printed in China

14 15 16 17 [TIMS] 5 4 3 2 1

www.thomasnelson.com

DEDICATION

Thanks to my loving wife, Suzanne,
and my four dear children,
Sellers, McCullough, Worth, and Emerson,
who give freely of their time, love, and resources
so I can help others pursue their dreams.

I have been crucified with Christ and I no longer
live, but Christ lives in me. The life I now live
in the body, I live by faith in the Son of God,
who loved me and gave himself for me.

GALATIANS 2:20

Contents

Foreword

My friend Dr. Morris Pickens ("Dr. Mo" to me) has been a great help to me as I prepare for tournament play.

That may not sound like much to you, but for my career, it's pretty much everything. If I'm not prepared—fully, completely, confidently prepared—to go head to head with the greatest, most gifted, and skillful golfers in the whole world from week to week, then I may as well hang it up and find another job.

There's nothing wrong with another job, but for this one relatively brief chapter in my life, I have the privilege of playing on the PGA tour, experiencing competition at the highest level I can imagine. While I'm here, while the opportunity is before me, I want to maximize it. I want to be the best I can be.

Preparation isn't a luxury on the tour; it's life support. It's everything. As Fred Couples used to say, "When you're prepared, you're more confident. When you have a strategy, you're more comfortable." I want to be prepared, and I want to have a strategy—in golf *and* in life.

With Dr. Mo's help, my practice times have become more productive. Good practice doesn't necessarily mean you have to go out there and work from sunup to sundown seven days a week. Preparation doesn't necessarily mean more practice; in my case, it means *smarter* practice. In short, it demands a strategy.

Dr. Mo has helped me to recognize some areas of deficiency in my game, and he has designed some incredibly helpful personalized drills and practice methods to enable me to improve in these areas. In fact, some of the drills he gave me on chipping and putting helped me to win the Masters in 2007.

As you will discover in the pages of this book, Dr. Mo's greatest strengths are his knowledge of the short game, putting, and the pre-shot routine.

Don't look down on that little word *routine*. I know that it might not sound too exciting, but having a sound pre-shot routine—a consistent and productive way to manage my emotions and control my thought process around the ball—in my career is the difference between success and failure, between winning tournaments and sitting in some coffee shop somewhere reminiscing about "what might have been."

But please hear me on this: all of the training and drills and routines in the world won't count for much if my personal world is coming unraveled. I not only need a process for golf but I also need a process for *life*. If I occasionally win big checks on the tour but lose my wife and my family and the respect of my colleagues and friends, what have I gained?

I'm especially happy to recommend Dr. Mo's book because it's about winning at golf—and at life as well. He's right when he says that we need a strategy for both. Championship-level golf doesn't happen by accident, and neither does a happy, satisfying, productive life.

We need a plan.

We need God's help.

And we need friends like Dr. Mo who set a strong example and lead the way.

ZACH JOHNSON
St. Simons Island, Georgia

Acknowledgments

A number of people had very strategic roles in enabling this book to become a reality, and I would like to recognize them for their contributions.

Scott Lehman for being the catalyst that got this adventure going. Without Scott, this book never would have gotten off the ground.

Jack and Marsha Countryman who oversaw the entire project from beginning to end and, in essence, shepherded me every step of the way.

Larry Libby and his wife, Carol, for taking my thoughts and ideas and turning them into meaningful sentences and paragraphs. Larry you are a wonderful communicator!

Lisa Stilwell for editing, design, and completion of the book. You are the best "polisher" I have ever known.

Tim Brown for countless hours of photography and editing.

David Yarborough, Jim Kay, and the staff at St. Simons Community Church for giving the writing team a warm and inviting place to meet so the project could unfold.

Steve Temmer and Mark Fritchman for their critical analysis and review of earlier manuscripts. Your input was extremely insightful and valuable. Thanks!

Bill Hughes and his staff for allowing us to use TPC Sawgrass, and Adam Mersereau and his staff at the PGA Tour for allowing us to take pictures during The Players Championship, 2013.

My mom and dad for their continual love, support, encouragement, and wisdom. And my other parents, Bubbie and Bop, for being great role models in so many different ways the last twenty-five years. Each of you has been an incredible blessing to me!

Dan Pruitt, Cubby Culbertson, Bill Jones, and a whole host of other men in Columbia, SC who got me started on this wonderful walk in the early 2000s. It's impossible to express the gratitude I have for y'alls love and guidance getting me started.

And finally, but most importantly, the players who helped me write the book. I'm grateful for your time and generosity in completing all of the interviews, pictures, edits, and so forth. Without each of you, there would be no book. Y'all are THE BEST!

INTRODUCTION

One Shot at a Time

If your head is in the wrong place, you
can expect everything else to follow.

—Dr. Mo

From the *New York Times*, April 8, 2007:

Augusta, Ga.—The wind had finally eased at Augusta National Golf Club, and Zach Johnson, the son of a chiropractor from Cedar Rapids, Iowa, stood behind the 18th green not exactly sure what to do.

Tiger Woods, the last golfer with a chance to catch him, was still playing in the gloaming of the 71st Masters, so Johnson leaned in to hug his wife, Kim, and planted a kiss on the forehead of his 14-week-old son, Will, refusing to let go for several seconds.

"I was an emotional wreck," Johnson said. "I was a slob. I knew there were still chances for guys to make birdie."

When Woods stalled with three closing pars, though, Johnson had completed a task where 95 other golfers failed, claiming a Masters title after one of the most difficult weeks in the history of the tournament.

Johnson, 31, fired a closing three-under-par 69 on Sunday to defeat Woods (72), Rory Sabbatini (69), and Retief Goosen (69) by two strokes for his first major championship and second PGA Tour victory.[1]

Zach Johnson's head was in the "right place" almost the entire day on Sunday, April 8, 2007. And for the brief period that his mind wasn't in the right place, he paid the consequence on hole 17 with his only back-nine bogey.

Back in focus again on hole 18, he stayed in his process the rest of the way, winning the Masters and one of the most coveted prizes in the golf universe: the Green Jacket.

If it was a delirious moment for Zach and Kim Johnson, it was almost as much for me, Zach's coach and golf psychologist. Over the last nineteen years I have seen this pattern repeated countless times. Isn't it amazing how a little, white, dimpled ball will go wherever a skull-encased, two-hemisphere, gray-matter ball tells it to go?

When you are *thinking* your best, you focus on one shot at a time. There is no looking back or projecting forward. Thoughts of your score or what you might shoot do not exist. The implications of winning a tournament become as irrelevant as snowshoes in South Georgia. Mistakes from earlier in the round are completely forgotten. Your focus is *entirely* on the shot before you, and nothing else. When not playing your shot, your mind is consumed with the simple joys around you: the smell of the grass, the beauty of the clouds, a conversation with your playing partners. You're not thinking about the next hole or how the match stands or why your last shot landed between a willow and a pine. You are in control of your mind, and your focus is clear and concise. The million-dollar question is (and for my students, that million dollars may be literal), "How do you keep your mind this focused every time you play?"

In golf I believe your best chance of achieving this focus is *to have a thinking process that occupies your mind.* This process gives you the best chance of playing at a higher level more often.

It's strange how some high-achieving businesspeople closely follow tried-and-true processes in sales, marketing, and medicine but step onto the golf course with only a hope and a prayer and a vague plan to "try to do better today." And maybe they'd best forget about the prayer part too. Even Billy Graham once said, "The only times my prayers are never answered are on the golf course."

If a process helps to sell cars, market soda, or treat illness, it will also have value for your day on the golf course. The key is to make your thinking process (1) effective and (2) a habit of mind. Make it as much a part of your game as your swing off the tee or a blast out of the bunker.

In my opinion, all great players utilize a consistent thinking process. And even average golfers—weekend golfers—use such a thinking process when they're playing their best.

What is this productive process for improving your golf game?

I call it the 4-Rs.

And when consistently applied, the 4-Rs produce the fifth R, *results*. For my students, that may mean joining an elite company of those who conquer a major tournament on the tour. In fact, my students have twenty-three PGA tour wins since 2005, and three have won majors.

For golf hobbyists who simply love the game, it will mean the sweetness and satisfaction of playing at a level they had only dreamed of. And that is no small thing.

It's like when you meet your retired neighbor on the way to the mailbox and something in the brief conversation reminds him of a golf game long ago and far away on a day when he couldn't seem to miss. "I tell you," he says, waving a stack of bills and junk mail in the air, "everything I hit went into the hole. It was windy as anything that day, and the rain was in my face. But I forgot all about the weather and played the best game of my life. I think I must have shot 77. Now *that* was a day!"

That's how we remember those golden days when we maintained our focus through eighteen holes—or most of them—and found ourselves more into our game than ever before. What follows in these pages, then, is a process that will surely get you there more often.

The 4-Rs, in order, are:

1. **REFOCUS**. This is your golf *decision making* and involves shot selection, club selection, lie, wind, obstacles, and the best place to advance the ball. This is when you should be doing the vast majority of your thinking on the course, and it occurs *behind* the ball before you walk into the shot.
2. **ROUTINE**. The pre-shot routine is your golf *preparation* and includes how you walk in, get set up, and take practice swings if desired. This

happens only after the decision has been finalized, and it occurs walking *into and beside* the ball but before you actually swing.

3. **REACT.** This is your golf *execution*—making the actual swing or stroke. This happens *immediately after the routine is done* and can best be described as the player's "trusting and going."

4. **RELAX.** This is your *relaxation* on the course and speaks of how you spend time *between shots,* when you release your focus on golf. During this time you can think about architecture, wildlife, clouds, hobbies, anything—just not golf. Surprisingly, the overwhelming majority of your time on a golf course is spent on the fourth *R*, or at least it should be!

For this process to improve your score, it must become a consistent part of your game, not an "add-on" when you feel it is needed. It is *always* needed.

The fact that golf happens to be an excellent metaphor for life shouldn't surprise us. If the sport had been around in the first century, no doubt the apostle Paul would have used it in his New Testament letters. Instead, he used the sport that did occupy the minds of sports fans two thousand years ago: running races in the Olympics.

Israelite and Pharisee that he was, can there be any doubt that Paul was a sports fan? To the Corinthians he wrote:

> Do you not know that in a race all the runners run, but only one gets the prize? Run in such a way as to get the prize. Everyone who competes in the games goes into strict training. They do it to get a crown that will not last, but we do it to get a crown that will last forever. Therefore I do not run like someone running aimlessly. (1 Corinthians 9:24–26)

Paul even got the sport of boxing in the mix, adding, "I fight to win. I'm not just shadowboxing or playing around" (1 Corinthians 9:26 TLB).

But it was to the church at Philippi that Paul gave the best advice for golf—and life. After explaining his goal of experiencing the power and presence of Jesus Christ in a fresh and life-transforming way, he went on to say:

> Not that I have already obtained all this, or have already arrived at my goal, but I press on to take hold of that for which Christ Jesus took hold of me. Brothers and sisters, I do not consider myself yet to have taken hold of it. But one thing I do: Forgetting what is behind and straining toward what is ahead, I press on toward the goal to win the prize for which God has called me heavenward in Christ Jesus. (Philippians 3:12–14)

That's it. That's one of the irreplaceable keys to golf—and life: "Forgetting the past . . . looking forward to what lies ahead . . . press on . . . to win the prize." The key to golf is playing one shot at a time. The key to life is living in the moment.

Golf is life. If you can't take golf, you can't take life.

—AUTHOR UNKNOWN

As Stewart Cink says, "Glorifying God on the golf course doesn't mean playing the greatest golf you've ever played; it just means being every bit of the golfer you can be on any given day."[2]

Likewise, Zach Johnson says, "Golf is a game of staying in the *now*."

When you think about it, what's the alternative? You can't play Friday's round on Thursday, and you can't tee off on the 18th if you're in the bunker on the 16th. But you can grasp the incomparable privilege of stepping behind the ball for this one solitary shot and, using every bit of the talent God gave you, maximize the investment of all those who believed in you, helped you, taught you, and encouraged you along the way. This you *can* do.

Jim Elliot, a young missionary martyr who was slain by Auca warriors on the banks of Ecuador's Curaray River in 1956, once expressed it like this: "Wherever you are, be *all* there. Live to the hilt every situation you believe to be the will of God."[3]

We can't do anything to change the past, and the future doesn't even exist yet. What does exist is this day, this hour, *this moment*. And how you live in the right now—the focus, energy, discipline, perspective, and wisdom you bring to this day, this solitary square on the calendar—will determine your future, your legacy, and your destiny.

I call this the 4-Rs. Paul called it "press[ing] on toward the goal" (Philippians 3:14). Jim Elliot called it living life to the hilt. Whatever you call it, it's a beautiful way to do golf—and just about everything else you have ever valued.

CHAPTER 1

Refocus: Regaining Your Direction

You swing your best when you have
the fewest things to think about.

—BOBBY JONES

Stewart Cink and I had been working together for only a few months in 2009 before he had the opportunity to play at one of the crown jewels of golf: the British Open. The oldest championship tournament in golf, it was being played that year at what may be the world's original golf resort in Turnberry, Scotland.

I would love to have been there. What golfer wouldn't? It's not only the undulating greens, the ocean-hugging views, and the sight of the Ailsa Craig rising up out of the whitecaps and misty blue on the Firth of Clyde. Scotland, after all, is the very birthplace of golf, sometime back in the fifteenth century. Hoisting your golf bag and walking across the Scottish links is something like backtracking a winding river all the way upstream to the headwater springs high in the mountains.

Besides all that, I would like to have been there for Stewart's sake, giving him whatever encouragement or advice that I could in his first major since we started working together.

The year 2008 and the first few months of 2009 hadn't been very satisfying for Stewart, and it showed in his results. His best finish was twenty-fourth at the limited-field Mercedes-Benz Championship in January, and he had missed the cut in the first major, the Masters. That showing in particular and his overall poor play were beginning to have an impact on his thinking.

Watching his first nine holes at the Players Championship that year, I knew exactly how I could help him if he ever asked. His problem mostly had to do with his putting. He clearly had no set pre-shot routine, and he wasn't confident at all walking into his putts. There was a lot of "wishing" going on when the putter was in his hands. In short, he had lost his way on the greens.

On May 17, after Stewart had missed the cut at the Players, I got a call from him.

"Hey, Mo," he said, "are you ready for a serious project?"

I couldn't help but smile. "Stewart," I said, "this is the project I've been hoping to get for over a year. And it's not nearly the project you think it is. You're a lot closer than you realize!"

It was with that brief interaction that our working relationship officially got started, and I couldn't have been more excited. I made plans to meet with Stewart on the following Tuesday, and we got right down to business on the greens.

Just a few weeks after that, Stewart left to play in the British Open. What an outstanding opportunity for him—or for any golfer. Speaking of the British Open, Lee Trevino once said, "To me, the Open is the tournament I would come to if I had to leave a month before and swim over."[1]

But I didn't have a month right then to make the swim, and I couldn't be there to offer any counsel. All I could do for my friend was pray for him and text him what I hoped would be a strong reminder of what we had worked on together—especially on the greens. My message to him was, *"Invite the challenge."*

He knew exactly what I meant. In the brief time I had worked with Stewart, I knew that he tended to view big tournaments as burdens to be endured rather than as challenges to be relished. I had told him the very reason you turn pro, try to get on the PGA tour, and take on some of the legends of golf is because you *want* the challenge. You're doing exactly what you want to do and what untold thousands of aspiring amateur and weekend golfers long to do but may never have the opportunity to do. So when the big moments come, you want to relish them.

And this was the biggest golf moment that thirty-six-year-old Stewart Cink had ever faced. He needed to invite the challenge, invite the pressure, invite the competition, and step into it with all his heart. And of all the mental tools we had been discussing to improve Stewart's competitive mind-set, the concept of REFOCUSING might be one of the most important tools of all.

For many golf fans around the world and for the assembled media at Turnberry, the British Open that year was more a story about what *could have* happened rather than what did happen. What had everyone so excited was the apparent comeback of the legendary Tom Watson, who was fifty-nine at the time and on the cusp of pulling off what many might have regarded as one of the greatest wins in the history of the game. Watson had won five British Opens from 1975 to 1983 and was making a strong run at the 2009 Open.

He had opened with a blistering 65 and followed the next day with a 70 to move into a tie for the lead. In the third round he shot 71 to take the lead, and in the final round he had held or shared the lead for much of the day. Stewart Cink, however, was right there with him—a very tall shadow (at 6' 4") that would have been difficult to ignore.

On that final round, it really all came down to a 15-foot putt on the 72nd hole. If Stewart could nail that putt, he would find himself 2-under and "leader in the clubhouse"—the player with the lowest score having completed regulation play. Writing about that putt after the tournament was over, a reporter at *Golf Digest* called it "a breakthrough moment."

And this was the point where Stewart very much needed to remember the first of the 4-R principles we'd been working on together. He needed to REFOCUS before he stepped behind the ball to attempt that putt.

Stewart later described the moment like this:

> Okay, so you've got 15 feet between you and the hole. Obviously, there is a physical side and an emotional side to that putt. It feels a little different when you're 15 feet away on the final hole with a chance to beat Tom Watson and win a major than it does when you're on the practice green warming up

with your friends. Yes, it's still 15 feet, but it *feels* different. You wouldn't be human if you didn't feel some emotion. You know you're "in the hunt" to win your first major. You know what it would mean to *make* that putt, and you also know what it would mean to *miss* that putt. When you're in that kind of situation, the normal human tendency is to try to steer or guide the ball into the hole, instead of just following through on your routine.

We spend a lot of time in our practice, however, trying to reduce the putt into its basic physical meaning. It's so many feet . . . it's left or right. These are the physical attributes that don't change much from green to green.

However . . . this was the fabled Open. People all over the world were watching. This was a duel with one of the all-time greats of the game, one of Stewart's personal heroes, and a golf warrior who himself had

> The refocusing step is when you do the majority of your "golf thinking" on the course.

dethroned Jack Nicklaus. This was a purse of $1,221,005. This would be his first victory in a major. This would be a mountaintop in his career no matter what followed.

How do you put such things out of your mind?

The answer is, you don't. No one can. Golfers are human beings, not robots, and no one truly knows how to consistently blank thoughts out of the conscious mind on command like a child with a magic slate. But you also remember that while golf has its emotional side, it has its physical side as well. So what do you do in such moments? You simply acknowledge that the shot has special meaning, do your best to set that aside, concentrate on all the physical aspects of the putt, and make a stroke.

And that's what Stewart did. He tipped his hat to all the what-ifs, set them aside, refocused on the physical putt before him, stepped into the ball, and put it in the hole. As history will recall, that birdie forced him into a four-hole playoff with Tom Watson, which Stewart won by six strokes. And in a brisk wind rolling across those venerable greens and creating whitecaps on the sea, he hoisted the fabled Claret Jug trophy.

In a postround media interview, Stewart told a British journalist, "Extraordinary. It's been a surreal experience. Playing against Tom Watson, this just doesn't happen. I grew up watching him and hoping I could follow in his footsteps." Speaking of the British Open, he said, "I'm happy just to be a part of it—let alone win."[2]

Stewart could well say that, even though most of the gathered media had been pulling hard for fifty-nine-year-old Watson to win the day. When Watson walked into a somewhat glum and defeated media room after Stewart's surprise win, the old pro joked, "Hey, this ain't a funeral, you know."[3]

Let's take time to look more closely at this first of the 4-Rs, the one that helped Stewart overcome some of the difficulties of his game—and within weeks claim one of golf's most coveted titles. It's what I call the REFOCUS step.

Every one of us brings worries and concerns and distractions to the golf course.

Why?

Because we bring *ourselves* to the golf course.

As human beings, most of us are always dealing with a dozen things at once—our marriage, our finances, our kids, our needed house repairs, our work, our upcoming vacation, our health concerns, and on and on.

One of my professional golfer students right now has a wife who is pregnant and getting closer to her due date. Does he bring that with him into his tournaments? Of course he does. He loves his wife and is concerned for her. But once he walks on the course, the most important thing he can do for his wife and his family is to focus on his game and reap the rewards of all those countless hours of practice and drills.

Sometimes I'll tell one of my students, "If something's on your heart, write down your concerns in a notebook or record them on a little digital recorder, and then put them in your locker. They'll be there waiting for you after the round, and you can pick them up. But right now the best thing you can do for your family is to use your gifts and abilities to go compete your tail off."

If my student thinks about his pregnant wife in the middle of the round, that's okay. But he needs to learn a process that will allow him to acknowledge

the issue, acknowledge the emotions, and then set them aside and move back into the process he has adopted.

That's where refocusing comes in.

You refocus before a round of golf, and you refocus before every shot on the golf course. In the midst of your game, "refocus" refers to how you process all the relevant information before you attempt to play the upcoming shot. Refocusing occurs after you have relaxed from the previous shot (or after your warmup for the first shot of the day) but before you begin your pre-shot routine. The refocusing step is when you do the majority of your "golf thinking" on the course. It's the moments in a competitive round when you "tune back in" to your game.

The primary action of refocusing is to make a decision about your upcoming shot.

Usually this "tuning back in" will start to occur about five to ten steps before you get to your ball. You don't really need to start refocusing much before this, because the physical environment around your ball will dictate your preparation and game plan for the next shot.

If you're riding in a cart, relax (I'm serious!) until you come to the ball, tee box, or green. Once you take a club out of your bag, let this be your signal to start refocusing.

There are many different checkpoints, or variables, you will want to consider when you refocus to play your next shot. These include, but aren't limited to, the following:

- lie of the ball
- yardage to the pin or target
- wind
- uphill or downhill
- pin placement
- slope of the green
- risk/reward assessment
- altitude
- location and severity of any hazards
- any other obstacles

Assessing these variables will help you make a decision about your next shot. (*I will use* this *club, hitting the ball in* this *way, to get to* this *location.*) These are the physical facts about a given shot or putt that will help you to set aside the distracting, emotional thoughts that may be trying to crowd their way in and occupy your mind. You may not be able to banish those thoughts completely, but please hear this: *you can crowd them out with all the physical aspects of the shot you'll be making in just a few moments.*

At this point in your process, you're like a chess player looking at the players on a chess board. You're trying to see the situation exactly the way it is, notice all the variables, and decide on your next move.

The refocusing step is over only after you have made a firm decision on exactly the type of shot you will play. Then it's time to move behind your ball and start your pre-shot routine. If you're still trying to decide what you want to do and you are already into your routine, you need to stop, back off, and refocus again before starting your routine over. Don't worry about others who may be watching you. Don't concern yourself with how it might look to step back and refocus. It's the wisest move you could make in that moment. *Decision making occurs during the refocusing phase, not during the routine.*

As I mentioned earlier, when I first started working with Stewart Cink, his putting game had fallen off, he'd become inconsistent, and it bothered him *a lot*. He was very emotional about it. And of course, as you can imagine, the more emotional you feel about something like that, the worse the problem becomes.

My challenge with Stewart was to reduce the action of putting to its bare physical elements and remove the emotion and drama from the process. I told him, "You've got to start making all of your putts in the same way, and how you will accomplish this is to make them all physical. Every putt will have three parts: distance, slope, and break or curve."

So after we worked on this, he would literally walk up to every putt and go through this three-part litany: "This is 20 feet, downhill, and breaks left to right." Or, "This is 8 feet, uphill, and straight."

Not only will such thinking set you up to perform your best, but it will also replace the emotional thoughts that try to fill your mind and define the putt for you. Consider, for instance, the following emotional pre-putt thoughts: *This is 8 feet for birdie . . . to get to 2-under . . . so I can stay one inside the cut line . . . so I can make money this weekend . . . so I can pay my upcoming mortgage.* Do you hear all the emotion and drama? That's five emotional statements in a row, and they're all being loaded onto a physical action that will take about three seconds. As a result the sheer physical aspects of making the putt get crowded out. And the likelihood of making the putt gets lower and lower.

Another one of my students, Nick Watney, talked about the difference refocusing meant in the same tournament on the same hole on successive days. In the Saturday round of the 2011 WGC-Cadillac Championship in Doral, Florida, he double-bogeyed the 18th hole—and felt his chances of winning the tournament beginning to slip away.

"I'd been playing so well," he said. "In fact, I think I was tied for the lead." But then frustrations began to mount for the twenty-nine-year-old Watney. "I had just missed birdie putts on *both* 16 and 17, and felt really frustrated. As a result, by the time I got to 18, I wasn't mentally on that hole." In fact, his mind was back on the two birdies that had gotten away from him. How could he have squandered those opportunities like that? When would he get another chance like this? He'd known of golfers who had once come close in a big tournament—a world golf event or a major—and then never, for the rest of their careers, come close again.

What's more, the 18th hole at Doral was nothing to trifle with. In an article on Golf.com, the writer called the par 4, 467-yard hole one of "the hardest 18 holes in golf." With bunkers and palm trees to the right and water to the left, the tee shot demands an undistracted mind and a golfer following a disciplined routine.

At that moment Nick Watney had neither. As a result he hit a poor tee shot into the water and ended up making a double bogey.

Disappointed and upset, Nick met with me and his caddie, Chad, that night, finally calmed down, and regained his focus and composure. And kept it!

The next day he came to that very demanding tee shot at the same difficult hole—the "fairway pinched by tangled rough and water, followed by an approach to a water-guarded green"[4]—with a one-shot lead.

This time, however, Nick focused on the physical aspects of the shot, which effectively crowded out all other competing thoughts from his mind.

"I literally remember saying to myself, 'I'm right here. I'm on the 18th hole. This is it. There is nothing more important than this. I have to be in this moment right now—because this is all that counts. And I *am* going to pure this tee shot.'"

As it turns out he did hit a great tee shot and made birdie on the hole. Nick ended up shooting a five-under-par 67 that Sunday to win by two on a course so difficult it has been dubbed "the Blue Monster."

"How I handled myself and played that hole," said Nick, "might be the most satisfying feeling I've ever had a on a golf course."

LIFE APPLICATION

A Fresh Commitment to Seek the Lord

Learning to refocus may be the most important skill you will ever attain. If it helps in golf, it helps a thousand times over in life. That's because losing focus in golf shows up on a scorecard, a piece of paper relevant for one day; losing focus in life could change your marriage, your family, your career, your destiny.

My friend and student John Rollins described it like this:

In golf sometimes, maybe after a couple of victories, you're tempted to think you've got the game beat. You've got it all figured out. You've got it all under control. And then all of a sudden, it jumps up and bites you. It's the same in our walk with the Lord. The world is full of temptations and evil things—forces that are always trying to knock you off course. You think you've got life going, with everything right where you want it, and—boom—something happens. An illness. An injury. A bad decision. It jumps up and smacks you in the face, and it feels like you're starting all over again, and that you're a long way from the man you thought you were. Both golf and life in Christ demand our constant attention to stay on track.

The primary action of refocusing in life is simply making a decision to seek the Lord every day—and even many times throughout your day, and allowing Him to reset your thoughts, or renew your mind (Romans 12:1–2).

Making a decision—and keeping it—is a *commitment*. And a person is only as strong as his or her commitments. Everything that is best in life, everything that is worth keeping when the chips are down, grows out of a commitment, a promise. If you have something in your life that you're not really committed to, I can assure you of this: eventually it will fall out of your life altogether. A commitment to improve your golf score is one thing. Far, far more important is your commitment to your spouse, your children, and your extended family and friends.

And infinitely more important than even these is your commitment to God. If you daily lock your focus on Him from the time your feet hit the floor in the morning, it will change you more than you could have imagined.

The apostle Paul described this process well in his letter to the church in Philippi. Paul was writing from a Roman prison at the time, which adds even more weight to his words:

Rejoice in the Lord always. Again I will say, rejoice! . . . Be anxious for nothing, but in everything by prayer and supplication, with thanksgiving, let your requests be made known to God; and the peace of God, which surpasses all understanding, will guard your hearts and minds through Christ Jesus.

Finally, brethren, whatever things are true, whatever things are noble, whatever things are just, whatever things are pure, whatever things are lovely, whatever things are of good report, if there is any virtue and if there is anything praiseworthy—meditate on these things. . . . and the God of peace will be with you. (Philippians 4:4, 6–9 NKJV)

Paul says that we can come into any situation in life with a tranquil mind, a peaceful heart, and an attitude of joy regardless of difficult or distracting circumstances. Very carefully and very specifically, he says, "Be anxious for *nothing*," and he says to bring "*everything*" to the Lord in prayer. Someone will say, "That would mean I'm praying all day long!" It might! It might mean you have a prayer going in the back of your mind as you move through your day, as you seek to turn every worry, every concern, every disappointment, and every setback into a prayer and then leave them with the Lord.

One of my favorite Bible characters is David, the nation of Israel's greatest king and a man who wrote at least seventy-three psalms, many of them about how to seek God. In Psalm 27:4 he wrote, "One thing I ask from the LORD, this only do I seek: that I may dwell in the house of the LORD all the days of my life, to gaze on the beauty of the LORD and to seek him in his temple."

As a warrior, a king, a father, and a husband, David had a lot going on in his life and a great deal to think about on any given day. But his strong commitment through it all was to seek the Lord in every situation.

Let me ask you this: Every day when you wake up, what do you seek? Is it money? Getting ahead on the job? Making a name for yourself? I know that I have wrestled with all of those desires.

If left to ourselves, we will just naturally focus on ourselves. We'll get caught up in our own wants and desires and plans and goals, and in the end, we'll be miserable for it and feel as empty as a discarded shell on the beach.

If you don't take time to refocus every morning, you won't "transform your mind." Instead, you'll keep thinking the way you always have and stay "conformed to the world." And as your day goes on, you'll end up like Nick Watney at the 18th hole of the Doral in the third round: frustrated, angry, unfocused, and unready to meet the challenges life throws at you.

What you want to do is to set aside the distractions, disappointments, and frustrations of your day, quit focusing on yourself, and seek the Lord's strength, stability, perspective, and joy as you walk into each of these situations with a composed mind and a strong sense of purpose to be the best spouse, parent, or friend you can possibly be.

CHAPTER 2

Routine: Maximize Your Preparation

The more I practice, the luckier I get.

—Ben Hogan

D usk fell swiftly in the desert as the sun set behind the mountains. It was October 2010 and there was a chill in the air and a stiff breeze—a perfect evening for football under the lights.

But this wasn't football; it was championship golf, and the three men who were still standing in the Justin Timberlake Shriners Hospitals for Children Open in Las Vegas had a decision to make. Australian rookie Cameron Percy, Scotsman and defending champion Martin Laird, and my student and friend Jonathan Byrd had already played three holes of a sudden-death playoff. But dusk was softening the edges of distant objects. Was there enough light left to play one more hole, or should they suspend play and come back on Monday?

The PGA official was leaving the decision with the men who had the most on the line. Did they want to continue play, even in twilight conditions? They all hesitated, knowing the high stakes at *this* Vegas table. But then they thought of the fans who had turned out to watch the tournament and had stayed with it all day, shot for shot, hole for hole.

They decided to keep playing. After one more hole, hopefully it would be decided, and the winner would walk away with a purse of $774,000.

The leaders had finished regulation play tied at 21-under, and after three playoff holes, it was still up in the air. Jonathan had thought he'd won the tournament on the second playoff hole—when a beautiful 25-foot birdie putt hit the hole, spun 180 degrees, and popped back out of the cup. The ball kept on rolling, down the side of the green toward the water. The gallery groaned, and in his mind Jonathan thought, *Well, that's that*. But after saving par—and watching his foes miss their birdie attempts, he was still alive.

After they had all parred the third playoff hole, the PGA official, looking around at the rapidly fading daylight, asked them if they wanted to go on. And they said they did.

Jonathan went first at that final hole. He took time to refocus, looking 204 yards down a fairway at a flag he could barely see in desert twilight. Selecting a 6-iron and adjusting his navy-blue Mizuno cap in the wind, he stepped behind the ball and, with no hesitation, went into his pre-shot routine.

That's the wonderful thing about it. You never know when simply pursuing that routine will lead to a situation that is anything but routine.

Even if you didn't watch the video of that shot, you could take in the scene by just listening to the Golf Channel announcers' voices, speaking in those hushed, muted tones that they use—that soon became excited shouts.

ANNOUNCER 1: The wind has really picked up here. Check out that flag. It's blowing pretty hard.

ANNOUNCER 2: Two birdies in regulation for Jonathan Byrd and . . . WHAT A SHOT! It's over! It's OVER. [laughter]

ANNOUNCER 1: Unbelievable! *How about this?* UNBELIEVABLE.[1]

Yes, Jonathan had made a hole in one to win the sudden-death tournament, something that had never happened before on the PGA tour. Until then. The ball hit 10 yards short of the hole and rolled in like a putt.

For a few moments Jonathan wasn't even sure what had happened. He not only didn't see the ball go in but could barely see the flag. There was some cheering, but not that much, from the few remaining fans standing on the distant green.

Dazed and incredulous, Jonathan turned to his caddie. "Did it go in?" he asked.

"It was kind of hard to process," Jonathan said later, "because I was still in shock."

After standing for a moment with his hands on his hips, peering into the distance, he stuck his tongue in his cheek, shook his head a little, and turned to Percy and Laird.

"Are you kidding me?" he said. In spite of their disappointment, both men gave Jonathan big smiles and enthusiastic high fives.

It was a stunning end to a difficult season for Jonathan. He had been 130th on the money list on the tour and had known he would have to play inspired golf in the last weeks of the season just to keep his card. He hadn't won a tournament since his victory at the 2007 John Deere Classic three years before. But now, on the strength of this win, he had a paycheck of three-quarters of a million dollars and a two-year exemption to stay on tour no matter what.

His first thoughts on making the hole in one, however, weren't on the big payday or the exemption. They were on the faithfulness of God.

If you work hard and faithfully at your routine and then simply execute that routine without allowing yourself to be distracted by possible failure or success, good things will happen.

"I literally had this thought," Jonathan told me. "I said, 'God, You brought me through this whole season when I've played so poorly, right up to this tournament when I didn't even know if I would make enough money to keep my card. Then I'm in the final group leading the tournament, and if I could have shot a 67 in that final round I would have won it outright. But instead, there was a playoff, and on the last hole, I made an ace. God, You have scripted this out better than I could have ever imagined.'"

The odd thing was that he simply had to take it in stride without celebrating. Cameron and Laird had yet to make their shots. "I didn't want to jump around on the tee, pump my fist, and act like an idiot," Jonathan said, "and that's not me anyway."

So he calmly stepped back to let his two dazed competitors hit their shots. He said, "Here you go, guys. Good luck. Knock it in the hole."

But they didn't. They both hit their shots into the water, and it's no wonder. Jonathan's shot had unnerved them. "You're never prepared for a hole in one," Laird later told the media.[2]

That's the way it is with this second of the 4-Rs. If you work hard and faithfully at your routine and then simply execute that routine without allowing yourself to be distracted by possible failure or success, good things will happen.

For Jonathan that very, very good thing happened to him after three years without a tour victory, as he dropped lower and lower on the money list. But he stayed with it. And on an improbable night in the desert, in failing light and a stiff wind, his routine suddenly brought him a rich and very encouraging reward.

Wasn't it just "good luck" to make an ace that evening? Perhaps, but as Ben Hogan once said, "The more I practice, the 'luckier' I get."

Was Jonathan in some kind of zone in that moment, allowing him to hit an extraordinary shot? Maybe. But as we all know, "zones" come and go, and many golfers can't tell you where they came from or where they disappeared to when they were needed.

I'm a sports psychologist and what you might call a technician of the game, but I don't have it in my power to put my students into "zones" where everything will fall exactly right for them. That really isn't my job. My job is to teach them a process that will get them right up to the door of that zone. Sometimes the door will open, and sometimes it won't. But it's my job to help get them to that door more often.

And that begins to happen as my students develop the crucial second *R* of the 4-Rs: their pre-shot ROUTINE.

A pre-shot routine is a sequence of mental and physical actions that precede the actual swinging of a club. The actions of your routine prepare you *mentally* and *physically* to play each shot. Your routine should start on the tee of the first hole (or the practice range, if you had time to warm up), and continue for each shot of an entire round.

There should be a very clear line, a complete separation, between the first *R*, REFOCUS, and the second *R*, ROUTINE. In other words, before you step into the ball, you should have already taken all the variables into account—wind, terrain, slope, and so on—and made your decision on how to play the shot. Your routine, then, is simply follow through to what you have already decided.

Don't start into your routine before your decision is finalized! You shouldn't be standing over the ball with the club in your hands still asking yourself, "Do I really want this club or that club? Do I really want that tree to be my target, or do I want that other one, just to the left?"

Questions like that have a way of short-circuiting your routine and won't give you the results you want. Answer all questions before you step into the ball!

A sound pre-shot routine is the very foundation for effective on-course self-management. I can't say that your routine is more important than the other three *R*s, but it is the area most likely to help you hold your round together should you have trouble with the other *R*s. *Simply put, if you don't have a consistent routine, you can't play great golf.*

Think back again to the story with which I began this chapter. Jonathan Byrd was a young man facing a moment of extreme emotional pressure. He had already felt emotional going into that tournament in Las Vegas. He'd played poorly through most of the season and watched his earnings drop like a rock. If he didn't play well in Vegas, he could have very easily been bumped off the tour—which would mean he would have to go through the whole process of requalifying. In his mind he could have recited the names of many good golfers who had fallen off the PGA tour and somehow never made it back again.

So his career was on the line, his pride was on the line, and his confidence was on the line. And at the most crucial moment, at the tipping point, he had to deal with a gusting desert wind and fast-falling twilight, making it difficult even to see the flag over the length of two football fields away from him.

What saved him in that moment, apart from the grace of God, was his *routine*. Because he had confidence in the routine he had developed and practiced over a period of years, he could step up to the ball without hesitation, swing his 6-iron—and make PGA history.

To develop your own individual pre-shot routine, it's important to think about a combination of two distinct routines, one *physical* and one *mental*. When effectively meshed together, these twin routines provide you with a relaxed focus, allowing you to hit good shots (if not necessarily holes in one).

YOUR PHYSICAL ROUTINE

You want to develop a physical routine that matches your personality. It should be what's easy and natural for you. Each of the professional golfers I work with has a great routine—but no two of them are just alike.

Think about other aspects of your life—your walk, talk, driving, and eating. Do you move quickly, or are you more laid back? Do you tend to be structured and organized, or are you more carefree? Let these other areas guide you in the development of your physical routine. *Your routine should flow and never be forced.*

What should your physical movements be, exactly?

I can't really tell you that in a book. As I mentioned, no two players I work with have the exact same pre-shot routine. I suggest you begin developing your routine by watching other players you like and see if an aspect or two of their pre-shot actions might work for you. I do, however, have a few routine guidelines that have proven to be very productive through the years.

- First, start your routine from a few steps behind the ball, and then move into a position parallel to the ball line and target. This will help you get a fuller, more detailed view of the shot.
- Second, your routine should include a rehearsal of the swing. This will help you stay loose and practice what you hope to accomplish in the swing. This doesn't have to be a *full* swing, although it can be.
- Third, your routine should also include a step to get properly aimed at and aligned with the target. Getting lined up incorrectly—to the left or right of your target—is a very easy habit to fall into. By making alignment a consistent part of your pre-shot routine, you can reduce the likelihood of this mistake occurring.

The process of developing your physical pre-shot routine will take time. Try a number of different ways and find one that feels comfortable to you. Remember, there's no "right" or "wrong" routine. It doesn't matter how many waggles or swings or looks you incorporate. Just do what feels best to you following the three guidelines above.

Actually practice *building* your routine. As a general rule of thumb, the total time to go through your routine, from finalizing the target behind the ball to actually making contact with the ball, should take about twelve to fifteen seconds. If your routine only takes ten seconds, that's okay. Allowing too much time gives you more time to have extra thoughts creep into your mind. Remember, you are trying to stay in the present, and having a routine that is too long makes this more difficult to achieve.

Practice your routine on the range and on the course. Don't expect to build a solid routine and make it happen quickly. You will probably make

revisions on a continual basis for your next ten to fifteen rounds until you settle into what is comfortable and what works.

Your routine, like a new wedge or new putter, requires time to get used to all the new "feels." Be patient and give it time to work. But remember, that's only half the story. It's every bit as important to develop a solid mental routine as well.

YOUR MENTAL ROUTINE

An effective mental routine, like its physical counterpart, also contains three components: *a very specific target, one positive swing thought*, and *commitment to the shot.*

1. SELECT A VERY SPECIFIC TARGET

This should be done from behind the ball. Picking a target before you start walking in to address the ball is important for two reasons. First, this gives you a finite starting point for your routine, making it easier for you to accomplish this important task in a consistent manner. Second, the target you choose dictates where you line up—and possibly even the type of shot you play.

How do you pick your target? I have two suggestions. First, *pick a target as small as your vision will allow.* This will give you the best chance of actually hitting the ball in the direction you desire. Picking a small target on the golf course is akin to someone shooting a bullet or an arrow at a target. If they aim at the bull's-eye, they give themselves the best chance of hitting it, even though it doesn't always happen.

Second, *select a target distinctive enough that you don't lose it in the surrounding environment when you look back down at the ball.* For example, instead of picking a single pine tree out of thirty that look just alike, pick a gap or hole in the group of trees—or perhaps a tower even farther away in the distance.

These guidelines for picking a target assume that a player is attempting to hit a straight shot. In golf, however, this rarely happens, as most players try to fade or draw the ball at least a little on most shots. If this is the case for some of your shots—if where you intend for the ball to end up is not where you need to start it to accomplish this—then you must in actuality have *two* targets. The first is where you want the ball to end up. We refer to this as the *actual target*. The second target is your *visual target*—what you need to aim at so that your ball will ultimately end up at your actual target. This visual target is the one that needs to be as small and distinctive as possible. After you select it, your visual target will be the only one you focus on. Your actual target and visual target will be the same only if you are attempting to hit a perfectly straight shot.

The last point I want to make about picking your visual target is that it should be at least as far away as your actual target. This tells your mind you are trying to maximize your distance for that shot. If you pick a visual target short of your actual target, it's possible to confuse your mind and hit it short of where you intended—simply because your visual target wasn't far enough to accomplish this.

Remember, your eyes tell your mind (and the rest of your body) where you want the ball to go, so it is very important to look at the proper target.

If you can't consistently accomplish this crucial step in your pre-shot routine, it is nearly impossible to play your best.

2. MAINTAIN ONE POSITIVE THOUGHT

The second step of your mental routine is to utilize one positive occupying thought throughout your routine. This can be a mechanical thought or a tempo thought, and it should be simple and easy to say to yourself. Most players' occupying thoughts come from tips or cues they get from their teachers during the course of a lesson.

This might be as simple as telling yourself, "Low and slow" or maybe "Smooth, smooth."

The reason it's beneficial to have a single, positive thought is that it simplifies your thinking and calms your mind. Remember, as I have already noted, you really can't think about "nothing." One popular marriage and family speaker claims that men (but not women) are able to go to a "nothing box" in their mind, where they literally think about *nothing*. It's just a big void, and when the wife asks her husband, "What are you thinking about?" he will turn to her with a blank look on his face and say, "Nothing. Nothing at all."

The speaker makes a humorous point here about the differences between men and women, but the real truth is, no one thinks about nothing. And that's especially true in golf. In any given round, there are literally hundreds of different things we can think about when preparing to hit a shot. *Is the club on the right path? Are my hands in the right position? Am I holding my hips still? Will I remember to follow through? Can I avoid the water up there on the right?* All of these are legitimate thoughts and concerns, but when they pass through your mind in the brief seconds before you begin your swing, your brain can't decide which one to focus on. In fact, you overload the switchboard! And as you bombard your mind with information, confusion sets in, and poor shots are the end result. To prevent this information

---

It's important always to tell yourself what you *want* to do, not what you *don't* want to do.

---

overload, it is crucial to *decide on one positive thought* and use it throughout your entire round.

You want to decide on only one occupying thought, because two or more thoughts may send conflicting messages to your brain. Your brain can't decide which is more important: to have a short backswing or a steady lower body. When you try to do both, you accomplish neither, and the result is a mediocre shot. If, however, you focus on only one thought—a positive thought—your brain is very capable of keeping that thought in focus and helping you to hit better shots.

You want the occupying thought to be positive, because the brain does a poor job of operating in the negative. For example, if you tell yourself, "Don't swing too fast," the brain has a difficult time deciding what you mean. It either doesn't pay attention to the word *don't*, and you swing too fast, or it overcorrects the problem and you actually swing too slow. The brain simply reacts better to positive messages when you are trying to perform. For this reason, it's important always to tell yourself what you *want* to do, not what you *don't* want to do.

The occupying thought you choose doesn't matter—*as long as it is singular and positive.* The reason it doesn't matter is because *its function is to block out other conflicting messages from entering your mind.* Telling yourself, "Turn-turn," may help you to make a better turn during your swing, but it may not. That doesn't really matter. What the thought *Turn-turn* is doing is keeping out *Don't block it to the right*, or some other distraction, and this is what is important.

As you go through your pre-shot routine, you will repeat your occupying thought several times to yourself. Exactly where you decide to include it will vary from player to player. Many players like to say their thought either as they are looking at the target or as they look back down at the ball. It will take some practice to find the sequence that works best for you. Although the occupying thought is singular, this doesn't mean it has to be one word.

Most likely your swing thought will be two to three words. Just remember to keep it positive and easy to repeat. Again, the key is to find something simple to say that will occupy your mind and minimize distraction.

In a casual round you can get away with not including a swing thought. However, when you are in competition and under the gun, this will be a critical part of the routine. If you wait to include it in competition and you haven't been doing it in practice, it likely won't help you—and may in fact hurt your performance. Practice it on the range and during each shot on the course. If you haven't been using your occupying thought in practice rounds, begin including it in advance of the tournament. This will be your best friend in competition when you need it the most.

A few paragraphs back I gave the example of two possible swing thoughts. But it really all depends on what your specific needs might be. For instance, your positive occupying thought might be, *Slow back*. Or maybe something as simple as *Short turn*. Right now I'm currently using "Short and drop." The exact words

> In my opinion, you can be in only one of
> three mental states when you hit a golf
> ball: *rushed, committed,* or *doubtful.*

you choose aren't important, but inclusion of a positive occupying thought in your routine is critical. Starting out, tempo thoughts (*Smooth, smooth*) are often most productive. But remember, while a smooth tempo is good, it isn't the primary objective of including an occupying thought in your routine. *The objective of including a positive thought in your routine is to occupy your mind so that it stays calm and focused and excludes other distracting thoughts.*

3. COMMIT TO YOUR SHOT

The third step of your pre-shot routine is to "look and react."

You've already made your *decision*; now your primary action is the *preparation* to play the shot. What you are trying to do here is to make sure you hit a committed shot, one that you are confident will go where you intend it to go. In my opinion, you can be in only one of three mental states when you hit a golf ball: *rushed, committed,* or *doubtful.*

A *rushed shot* is one in which you neglect to go through your entire routine, either physically, mentally, or both. It may be that you feel the shot isn't important or looks really easy. As a result you rush through your routine, either skipping parts of it or just not doing it. An example of a shot for which you might do this would be a layup on a par 5, a punch shot back out into the fairway, or a 2-foot putt. The next thing you know, you have hit the shot poorly and now have an extra shot to hit—or a shot that will be much more difficult than it would have been if you had taken time to go through your routine.

Stick to your process!

A *committed shot* is one in which you go through your entire routine and expect a good shot. You are totally confident that you are doing everything you can to hit the best shot possible. A committed shot may not necessarily turn out to be good—after all, we all make mechanical errors over time. But the key is that mentally you *expect* it to be good.

A *doubtful shot* is just that: one that is full of doubt or indecision. You aren't confident that you are going to hit a good shot, and yet you swing anyway! In golf, and even more particularly in life, never operate out of doubt.

It may be that you think you have the wrong club, or maybe you aren't sure about the type of shot you want to play, or maybe you simply aren't confident in your course management. Whatever the case may be, you hit a shot when you know you truly aren't ready. This is one of the absolute worst mental errors you can make in golf. Never, ever hit a shot if you have doubt about what you are trying to do. It's difficult enough to hit good shots when you know exactly what you want to do; it's close to impossible to hit good shots when you are swinging with fear, doubt, or indecision. If something in your routine doesn't feel right—or you get distracted by a noise or the wind or even a negative thought, *restart your entire routine.* Back off and do it again.

Yes, it's hard—or perhaps even awkward—to stop and restart. But continuing forward after something disrupts your routine is a sure invitation for disaster.

It may be that a car drives by and honks the horn as you are getting ready to hit your shot. Instead of backing off, however, you decide to "play through it." After you hit a poor shot, you are angry with yourself for not restarting your routine. If you know that you aren't ready, that something other than your occupying thought is in your mind, *you need to start over.* A good indication that you have actually hit a committed shot is when you look up and are surprised to see the ball going in the wrong direction. If, however, you find yourself saying, "I knew it!" and you aren't surprised to see it flying into the trees or the rough, you didn't hit a committed shot. At some point you expected to hit poorly. Going through your routine without being mentally into it isn't much of a benefit.

Remember, anyone can go through the physical motions of a pre-shot routine; players that end up winning are the ones who focus on their mental routine for each shot.

LIFE APPLICATION

A Consistent Walk Along the Right Path

Stewart Cink has learned the value of consistency. His key to success is very simple: "I try to stick with my routine. I make an effort to stay with my game."

Stewart has said that he gets ready for tournaments by trying to do the same things in the same ways no matter what the conditions.

> I try to prepare my ball flight to be a very neutral type of ball flight. Maybe the winds will be blowing really hard, or maybe the greens will be very soft. The fact is, conditions are always variable. Even so, I try to play in such a way that I don't have to alter my game very much. I try to be consistent day in and day out. Sure, the conditions affect what I do, but my goal is to remain the same, as much as possible, so that I don't have to make huge adjustments to my game all the time.
>
> It's the same thing in my life . . . in my Christian walk. I try to be the same person every day. I try to respond to situations in the same fashion, being true to myself, and true to my beliefs.

The key term here is *consistency*. It's walking with God day by day through life with a steady, step-by-step pace. That's why I like the term *walk* to describe the Christian life. It's not a sprint, and it's not a crawl. It is movement forward at a steady pace.

Some of the greatest heroes in the Bible made walking daily with God their most important routine in life.

I think of Daniel, a man from Israel who had been taken into captivity by the Babylonians when he was only a teenager. Through the years, remaining faithful to the God of his youth, he rose through the ranks of government service, first with the Babylonians and later with the Persian Empire.

At some point some jealous government officials who wanted to undercut and destroy Daniel found out that he went up to his room every day and in front of the open window prayed to God, facing toward Jerusalem. Seizing on this fact, they persuaded the king to make praying to God illegal, punishable by being thrown into a den of hungry lions.

The Bible says that when Daniel heard this news, "he went home to his upstairs room where the windows opened toward Jerusalem. Three times a day he got down on his knees and prayed, giving thanks to his God, just as he had done before" (Daniel 6:10).

Refusing to be upset, intimidated, or thrown for a loop by these threats, Daniel calmly stayed with his routine, following the Lord faithfully every day, just as he had for years. And when the crisis came and he found himself in the lions' den, God sent His angels to protect Daniel, and he went back to the routine that had never failed him.

From time to time you and I can find ourselves in a lions' den, too, facing challenges, dangers, problems, and threats beyond what we have ever faced before. How good it is in such moments to already have a routine of seeking God, praying daily, enjoying the friendship of strong fellow believers, and daily drawing comfort, wisdom, and perspective from God's Word.

It would be tough (let's face it, *impossible*) to develop a golf pre-shot routine when you're already in the midst of a major tournament. You might look for that "zone" in vain, and it would be too late to prepare. In the same way, finding God in a crisis may be difficult if you have no routine of seeking Him, talking to Him, and learning from His Word every day. At the very moment when you need God the most, you can't find His phone number. You don't know how to approach Him. You don't know what to say to Him. You don't have His wisdom to navigate your crisis.

Will He still hear your prayers and help you? Yes, He will. But how much better to already have an established habit and pattern of walking with Him when your marriage seems to be failing, when your wife has breast cancer, when your finances are tipping on the brink, when one of your teenage sons or daughters is walking on the cliff-edge of disaster.

Thinking back for a moment to Jonathan Byrd's hole in one, we realize that he never could have predicted the circumstances in which he found himself on that evening after sundown. He never could have guessed where

> Finding God in a crisis may be difficult if you have no routine of seeking Him, talking to him, and learning from His Word every day.

all his hard work and practice in developing his routine might take him: *to a single stroke that ended a playoff and a tournament and netted a three-quarter-million-dollar purse.*

But that's the way it is in life too. If you stay with your routine; if you walk the walk and keep on keeping on; if you stay faithful to your marriage vows, to your convictions, and to your God, you never know where your faithfulness will lead you. What's more, you may never know the benefits your family and friends will reap from your consistency. You might not see the results for years, when your sons and daughters have sons and daughters of their own. You might not even see the results in your lifetime.

But count on it, the results will be there. And it's not about you knowing the results anyway, because God knows.

Zach Johnson credits his daily routine of reading the Bible and talking to God with bringing calm and perspective to his life in spite of the ups and downs on the tour. "It's like my golf game," he said:

> The more I practice my putting or chipping or striking or whatever—trusting in the fundamentals, in the process, and in the drills, the more contentment and peace I have with those aspects of my game. In the same way, if I get in the Word every day, it just seems to bring about more peace and contentment. The more I get into it, the more I do devotions, the more

I'm learning and growing, the better off I am spiritually. It's not that I have the magic formula here or have all this nailed down—but I know what I need to do on a daily basis, and I know that contentment comes from consistency in my life.[5]

When I work with my students, consistency is one of the most important values I teach. You learn a great routine that works for you, you bring good techniques into your game, and then you seek to follow them *no matter what.* Rain or shine. Wind or calm. Heat or cold. Pressure situations or a Saturday round with your buddies.

If you are going to seek the Lord, then you'd better do it every day, because you never know what a day will bring. If you have an idea of making God a priority twice a year—on Christmas and Easter—you may not find His comfort, wisdom, strength, and help when you need it most, in the great perplexities and crises of your life.

In the pages of this book, I speak of several of my golfers who found great help in consistently playing their own game, even in the media spotlight and under incredible pressure. So it is in our lives.

In the Old Testament book of Amos, the Lord says to His people, "Do two walk together unless they have agreed to do so?" (3:3). God is willing to walk with you—right through the fire if need be. Are you willing to walk *consistently* with Him?

> If you are going to seek the Lord, then you'd better do it every day, because you never know what a day will bring.

CHAPTER 3

React: Trust and Go

Plan for a future day. Prepare for an upcoming day. Practice for a later day. But play for today.

—Dr. Mo

There are golf tournaments, and then there are golf tournaments.

In the life of a PGA tour player, the great tournaments keep rolling all year long. This year (2013) it began in January with the Hyundai Tournament of Champions at the Plantation Course at Kapalua, on Maui, and early in October will wrap up with the Presidents Cup at Muirfield Village in Dublin, Ohio. In between, there are dozens more battlegrounds, with storied names in stunning locations.

In the course of the year, there are also four major championship tournaments—the highest peaks in a range of towering mountains.

But one stands alone: the Masters at Augusta National.

There is an indefinable something about this tournament that sets it apart from all others in all other locations. Maybe it's because it's the first major each year, when everyone is getting back into golf after winter and football and basketball. Maybe it's because it's the only major played on the same course each year. I'm not really sure why, but for whatever reason, it is *unique*—"the Masters mystique."

"The winner of this tournament," Phil Mickelson said, "doesn't just win a major. He becomes part of the history of the game, and that's what excites me. The tournament creates something that is very special, and year in year out, history is made here."[1]

In 2007 my friend, neighbor, and student Zach Johnson had his opportunity at history. With a leaderboard that included Tiger Woods, Retief Goosen, and Stuart Appleby however, no one gave Zach much of a shot. But his Sunday round score of 69 tied the lowest score on the course and led to a two-stroke victory.

The life-changing victory was the result of many aspects of Zach's game coming together at the right time, but it was the third *R*, athletically REACTING, that really shined when everything was on the line. Here is how one key situation developed, including Zach's own memories of the day.

"It was the 72nd hole," he recalled, "I had a one-shot lead on Justin Rose, and I knew very well how important that hole was."

Yes, he'd certainly been in plenty of close finishes before. But this was a one-shot lead . . . in the final round . . . at *the Masters.*

There is an indefinable something about [the Masters] tournament that sets it apart from all others in all other locations.

Many golfers try to ignore or forget the leaderboard in the course of a tournament, but at that point, so near the end, Zach had to look. "There comes a point in the final round where you just have to look at the leaderboard. You have to know where things sit. I had a chip shot to make, and I knew that getting it up and down was extremely important."

Zach, however, had learned how to refocus, move into his routine, *and simply react to the shot in front of him.* Even so, it would seem only human, given the time and place, to let his mind stray to thoughts of the Green Jacket.

In fact, it never entered his mind. And it hadn't been until he was standing on the 16th tee in that final round that he turned to his caddie and asked, "Where do we stand? I probably need to know." His caddie informed Zach that he had a two-shot lead at that point.

A two-shot lead on the 16th tee! Was he thinking of the possible headlines that night if he won?

"No," he said, "I was still trying to compete. The thought of putting on the Green Jacket and all the rest of it wasn't even in my mind." (Zach tells me that my strongest message to him through the years has been "Compete, compete, compete.")

"Besides," he added, "I'd learned some hard lessons prior to that. Regardless of what you've got in front of you, whether it's a full shot, a chip, a ten-footer, or a one-footer, you've still got to keep playing and competing."

So Zach kept competing on 16, 17, and 18 until he found himself focused on the 72nd hole chip shot before him—and it wasn't what you'd call a "gimme." But he knew his routine for a chip and had practiced it for endless hours in all kinds of conditions. So without taking any extra time to agonize over the situation, he simply stepped into it and executed the shot.

"Looking back at the videos," he said, "it doesn't look like I was nervous, taking too much time, or even too quick. It just looked like I was in the mode of hitting a golf shot. I was able to go through my routine, go through the process of executing that chip shot in the same manner as if I was chipping on the very first hole. I was able in that moment to make that hole—the 72nd hole of the Masters—no more important than any other. I picked out my line, picked out where I wanted to land it, and just "armed" it down there . . . and it rolled to within six inches of the hole. For a moment, I almost thought I'd made it! Even though the round wasn't over, I felt like a weight had been lifted off my shoulders."

Golf commentator Martin Hall called it Zach's most memorable shot in the tournament. The man who had underwhelmed the media with his drives won the day with his short game.

One reporter phrased it, "Johnson did it the old-fashioned way. So much for the theory that the Masters is only for the big boys. Johnson didn't try to reach any of the par 5s in two all week, yet he played them better than anyone with 11 birdies and no bogeys."[2]

Zach's signature victory that day vaulted him from number 56 in world rankings to number 15—the first player outside the top 50 to win the Masters since they began keeping track.

In a golf sense, I think that his ability to simply and athletically *react* on the final hole made all the difference. But Zach didn't miss the chance to attribute his win to something beyond good strategy and golf skills.

"This being Easter," he told the media, "I cannot help but believe my Lord and Savior Jesus Christ was walking with me. I owe this to Him."[3]

Five years later, at the 2012 John Deere Classic in Silvis, Illinois, Zach demonstrated another classic reaction to an even more difficult shot than he had faced at the Masters. A reporter on the scene captured the sight with these words:

Johnson won the Deere on Sunday with a birdie on the second hole of a sudden-death playoff. His 193-yard 6-iron approach from the bunker left of the 18th fairway ran up to less than a foot from the cup for an easy birdie, enabling him to knock off *Troy Matteson*, whose approach landed 43 feet from the pin. . . . Zach Johnson already was a member of the board of directors of the John Deere Classic. Now he has another title at the tournament: champion.[4]

After teeing off on the 2nd hole of the sudden-death shoot-out, Zach had found himself squarely in the middle of the bunker, in a hazy dusk, with difficult visibility as he looked for the distant green. Zach, however, allowed himself simply to react to the challenging shot, stepped up to the ball, and went into his routine.

"I saw it bounce on the green," he recalled, "and hoped it would kick left. I couldn't see the golf ball."

But Zach couldn't miss hearing the roar from the gallery for the "hometown boy" as the ball rolled to less than a foot from the hole. (Zach is from Cedar Rapids, Iowa, about an hour from the Quad Cities.)

"When it comes to a playoff like that and you know you're in contention, you have to trust what you have already instilled in your game," Zach said. "That includes the walk up to your shot, getting your yardages, doing all the informational stuff, picking out your target, and then moving into your routine.

"That's *every* shot," Zach emphasized, "regardless of whether it's a drive, an iron shot, a pitch, or a putt. You have to rely on that, but you don't have to dwell on it. You do, however, have to remain athletic and have a feel for the game. I had a clear lie when I approached that bunker shot, so I just went through my routine. Looking back, it didn't feel much different than hitting my second shot on the 18th hole in my first round Thursday.

"Obviously, the result got my emotions going. It was dusk, and I couldn't see the ball. But I could hear the crescendo of applause, and that got me going!"

Zach probably couldn't hear the TV announcers, who were shouting, "Beautiful!" "Spectacular!" "Oh my goodness, what a shot! I think the entire Midwest just sat up and smiled."

REACT . . . AND YOUR MECHANICS

The term *REACT* has two meanings. The first meaning refers to the last part of your pre-shot routine: simply letting your eyes come back to the ball after the last look at your visual target and swinging the club.

Don't think about trying to hit the ball. Don't think about where it may end up. Simply let your eyes come back to the ball and react—swing.

Imagine playing a par 5 with which you are very familiar. This could be a hole at your home course or one where you played growing up. This should be a fairly easy hole yet one in which you almost always have to hit a third shot, because it's difficult to reach in two. I want you to imagine that you're about to hit the third shot on this hole after a good second-shot layup. Again, this is a pretty easy shot, physically and mentally.

You go through the motions of your pre-shot routine. But instead of just reacting to the target after utilizing your occupying thought, some other random thought pops into your head. In that moment, you're distracted and your reaction falters. That's the point where you need to stop, step back, and start the process all over again. REFOCUS . . . ROUTINE . . . REACT. It doesn't matter who might be watching, and it doesn't matter if other players make fun of you for "losing your nerve."

Restarting is the best thing you can do in that situation.

But let's say you don't restart. And because you don't, you end up hitting it fat with the ball landing well short of the green, possibly in a hazard.

Instead of a chance for a birdie, you make a double bogey because of your poor reaction to the shot.

Sounds familiar, doesn't it? We all have had this happen to us at some point. Even the best players in the world aren't immune to such errors. Mostly, it's a mental, rather than a physical error. And just to prove it to yourself, you drop another ball down, take one look at the target, and simply react to the shot. More than likely, it lands where you wanted the first one to land—but it doesn't count!

The mental error that you made was that you started thinking about the *results* rather than just reacting to the target. You started thinking about what you wanted or what you were trying to avoid. If you had backed off, recomposed yourself, and focused on your routine, the result would have been different.

The more consistently you can simply "look and react" (rather than looking, *thinking about the results*, and then reacting), the more consistently you will hit good shots and good putts. It's like I tell players when I am caddying for them: "Don't *try* to make that putt. Just go through your routine and let your body react. Then you'll make the putt."

This third *R* of the 4-Rs is a critical factor in taking your game from the practice range to the course. If you are a player who can stand on the range and just stripe every shot, one after another, and yet can't come close to hitting it like that on the course, it's likely because you don't let yourself just react on the course.

Somehow, in an actual round, something different happens. Your thinking changes.

Each shot becomes "more important," because now it isn't practice, now it's for score or money or pride. You care a lot more about how this turns out, so you really start trying. And it's a funny thing; you don't do as well. On the range, you were "just doing it" and it was working. But now when you are

---

*The more consistently you can simply
"look and react," the more consistently you
will hit good shots and good putts.*

---

trying, it isn't working at all! Your mind is getting cluttered with all kinds of different thoughts, your swing has lost the smooth rhythm it had on the range, and your frustration level increases with each poor shot.

When you were practicing, you were just practicing. But now you are thinking about the results, and that is changing your game. So what has happened? How could you possibly go from hitting it so well to so poorly? And even worse, how did it happen so quickly?

Here's the bottom line: You lost trust in your body's ability to react appropriately to the target. Reacting takes trust; reacting *is* trust.

On the range, likely because "it didn't mean anything," you were very relaxed and you trusted that you could hit the ball close to where you were looking, so you didn't even think about it! You just looked and reacted, and the ball really did go where you were looking. When you got to the course, however, and especially after you hit one or two poor shots, you lost that trust. *Instead of still reacting, you started thinking and trying. And those are two very different mind-sets.*

So far I have discussed reaction as it refers to the ability to trust in your mechanics, look at the target, and swing. But remember, I said *REACT* has two definitions. The second meaning is how you respond mentally, emotionally, and physically after you hit the shot.

REACT . . . AND YOUR RESPONSES

Let's say you hit a really good tee shot, and you know it right away. Immediately after contact, you get feedback from both the feel of the shot and where you see it going. It's headed up the left side of the fairway as you had planned, and from the sensation in your hands and arms, you know it has been hit solid. *This was a great shot!* Your immediate reaction is one of relief and joy. But what transpires in the next fifteen seconds to one minute will be crucial to your ability to continue hitting shots so well. How you react to the shot, to *any* shot, has a direct impact on how well you play as the round progresses.

You can't let one bad shot—or great shot—throw off your whole day!

As I mentioned earlier, your reaction to a shot automatically starts immediately after making contact with the ball. As you watch the ball travel, you already have some idea of how well the ball was struck and maybe even where it will end up. As soon as you know where the ball will end up (this may occur well before it finishes traveling or not until the very last roll of the ball), *you want to begin preparing yourself for the next shot.* This preparation begins with your effective reaction to the shot just hit.

If the ball went toward the target (a positive result), you want your mind and body to go to the next of the 4-Rs, RELAX. However, if your ball did not go toward the target (a negative result), *you must react in a productive manner right away.* Your usual reaction, if it's similar to most golfers, is to say something negative. This may be a sarcastic comment about how poor a player you are—or disbelief that you could make the same mechanical error that you just made on the previous shot. Your negative comment may be accompanied by a variety of physical actions, from simply slumping your shoulders to throwing a club. Emotionally, you may be angry, disappointed, embarrassed, or all of the above. These feelings may last for several minutes, and they may exist without any overt behavior, spoken or implied. If any of this describes your normal reaction, it is unproductive and detrimental to your future performance.

So don't go there—*you don't have to.*

A negative response to a shot or negative comments about the shot will pull you in a negative direction. Instead of reacting negatively (which may happen just out of habit), what you need to do is to establish *an immediate positive reaction.* Don't think of it as a "slice" or a "hook," but rather as a shot that went left or right of the target. Pretend that you are evaluating the shot as a computer would (for example, 10 yards left, 5 yards long), not as you are accustomed to ("Another awful hook!").

After your initial evaluation of and reaction to a shot that didn't go toward the target, go back and assess your mental routine. Make sure you

had a specific target, that you utilized your occupying thought, and that you "looked and reacted," hitting a committed shot. It's critical that you first assess your mental routine before assuming that a poor shot was caused by a mechanical flaw. If you immediately jump to the conclusion that a poor shot was the result of a mechanical error, you may be "fixing something that isn't broke." By going back through your mental routine first, you can get much better at determining the real cause of your poor shots. This isn't easy to do, because it takes a lot of willpower to admit that your mind, not your swing, may be the cause of your problems.

Think of it like a trip to the doctor when you're sick. If the doctor always treated the symptoms but never really got down to the *cause* of the symptoms, you might stay sick for a very long time, only masking the symptoms for brief periods after you changed medications. The same thing is true of your golf game. If you always blame the mechanics and never get down to the root of your problem—that your mental game is sloppy or that your attitude is negative—your golf game will remain "sick" also.

Up to this point, we have been discussing mainly negative reactions to poor shots and how you can change these to allow for better performance. But the same principle can be used for really good shots—your best shots— too. Overreacting to what just happened on the course, whether it puts you over the moon with joy or down in the pits with disappointment and disgust, will have a direct impact on your future performance. To be specific, the next shot or next hole.

As Ben Hogan was fond of saying, "The most important shot in golf is the next one."[5]

We all strive for peak performance. But what does that really mean? What it doesn't mean is a roller-coaster series of high highs and low lows. The fact

(Right) Zach putting with Titlist tour representative Jim Curran looking on.

is, peak performance doesn't happen on the mountaintop or in the valley. It is rather the result of pursuing the same productive principles over and over again. In other words, it is consistency that actually provides your best chance at peak performances. It's all about reacting in a consistent, productive manner, shot after shot, round after round.

Some players I work with get the idea that I never get upset or angry on the golf course. I'd like to make that claim, but, sorry, it isn't true. (I'm even worse at Clemson football games.) Like you, I have invested large amounts of money and time into my golf game. I'm as competitive as the next guy, want to win as much as anyone else, and can get emotional like anyone else.

Guess what? This is normal. We're H-U-M-A-N. We mess up, we fail to live up to our own expectations, and we get angry about it.

But here's the key. If you have a pencil or pen nearby, underline this next statement: *When you're angry about a shot on the golf course, get over it before the next shot.*

One technique that is very helpful in learning how to react properly is what I call the "emotion zone." You imagine a line or box that defines the space, or zone, where you allow yourself to react in a negative manner. Within the confines of this zone, you are free to do whatever makes you feel better emotionally—as long as it's within the rules. You can berate yourself, rip your glove off, slap your leg, sulk and moan, or say words that your mother would not have approved of. (Understand that I am "allowing" you [or myself] these reactions after a particularly bad shot or putt. And I'm certainly not advising you to let this emotional display become a habit!) All of this happens in that tiny box surrounded by imaginary yellow lines on the grass or around the bunker. *Once you exit the emotion zone, however, these negative reactions must be completely over.* You may even need to stop at the edge of the emotion zone to take a deep breath and recompose yourself before leaving that area. That's okay. The main thing is to get over it so that you can get prepared for the next shot. Period.

Where your mind goes, your actions will follow.

Your emotion zone might be the confines of a tee box. But once you walk out of that box (and step over that imaginary line), it's over. You're out of your emotion zone, you've left all negativity behind you, and you have moved on. Your "e-zone" boundary might be the fringe of the green or the edge of a bunker. It could also be 10 yards or so in the fairway, with the "exit" of the zone being a particular tree. (Can you see that sign in your mind's eye? EXITING EMOTION ZONE. Or maybe, YOU ARE NOW LEAVING THE EMOTION ZONE. HAVE A NICE DAY.)

You get the point. Once you cross that line, you leave your negative emotions behind. It's time to relax and enjoy the scenery, let your heart rate return to normal, and get yourself composed and ready for that next shot, which—who knows?—may be the best shot of your day.

Again, here's the principle: go ahead and enter the emotion zone if you absolutely need to, but don't stay there.

By the way, I'm not just talking here about red-hot anger or black depression or toxic cynicism. I'm also talking about mild disappointment, melancholy, "the blues," or minor frustrations. The truth is, even subtle reactions can have a direct effect on the rest of your performance. The human mind is a delicately tuned machine, and it doesn't take much to throw it off track. And where your mind goes, your actions will follow.

Remember this: one shot, no matter how excellent or terrible, will never make or break a round, but how you react to one shot may.

It's been one of the biggest lessons John Rollins has had to learn as we have worked together. "This is what I've really tried to work on this year," he said. "I'm trying to approach every day as its own day, whether I'm leading the tournament, in last place, in the middle of the pack, or wherever I am. I have a process to follow now, and I'm going to stick to that process. I'm going to trust it and believe in it. And I know that if I do those things, that gives me the best chance to play the best that I can on any given day."

Attitude and reactions to shots, John admits, are things he has struggled with from his first days on the tour. "I would always get too wrapped up with where I was in the tournament. If I was close to the lead, I'd get anxious and start thinking ahead—and bad things start to happen when you let those sorts of thoughts start creeping in." Similarly, if he found himself behind, he would battle with frustration, disappointment, and stress.

As John continues to practice the 4-Rs and learns to trust his routine more and more, he's finding more success leaving his emotions in a narrow, restricted emotional box and then walking out of that box into a more relaxed day on the golf course. "I want to be consistent," he said, "in the way that I think and in the way that I approach each day."

Zach Johnson agreed. "You have to go in and out of that emotion zone sometimes," he said. "You can't fight the fact that you are human. I would like to play unemotional golf—with no emotion whatsoever. That's especially true when you're at critical points of a tournament, with so much on the line. However, you have to embrace the fact that emotion is going to creep in here and there. So let it come, do what you're going to do, express what you're going to express, then put it aside and get back to living in the moment and playing your game."

LIFE APPLICATION

CONFIDENTLY ACCEPTING GOD'S PLAN FOR ME

Different golfers have different methods that help them with this crucial business of reacting to their shots.

For Stewart Cink it's an acronym he uses over and over again. I don't know if it would work for any other golfer on the tour, but it works for Stewart.

He calls it "GSAC," and it's as much a part of his golf game as his clubs. He explained it this way:

The G, he said, is for GLORIFY. He's a man who truly wants to bring glory to God in everything he does, on the course and off.

"Part of my job as a golfer," he said, "is to reflect Jesus Christ out there. That's a huge part of what I do. And the simple fact is, the better I can play, the more people will see that through me. Yes, there's pressure involved in that, but there is also a huge opportunity. My hope is that fans of the game or other golfers will be led to investigate the life of Christ and His grace for us because of the influence He has had on my life.

"My caddie and I talk about it every day before we walk from the range out to the first tee. I always stop and say, 'What are we going to do today? We're going to glorify His name.'"

But that doesn't necessarily mean the tally on the scorecard at the end of the day will be low. In fact, Stewart acknowledged that glorifying God in defeat is every bit as significant as glorifying Him in the big victories.

> "People are going to see how I *react*. People are watching how I respond and what I say, whether I shoot a 66 or a 79. There are parents and kids out there watching us play. There are volunteers who put in their time just for the love of the game—and sometimes you can make their day just by taking time to talk to them and be friendly with them.

"Yes, I would rather have the opportunity to glorify God on the days when I shoot 66, but there will always be those days when you don't play well at all. You still have to be responsible and remember who you represent out there. You can glorify His name on a bad day too. You don't always have to play your best golf, but you're still responsible to glorify Him."

The second letter of GSAC is *S* for SEGMENT.

"In golf," Stewart said, "that means I treat every shot as a unique circumstance. In other words, this shot that I am facing at this moment doesn't have anything to do with the one before it or the one that follows. Every shot is a brand-new ball game."

Isn't that a great concept? What if you lived that way? Instead of viewing a given Tuesday as just another day between Monday and Wednesday, what if you viewed it as an opportunity to live at your best? What if you set aside the days and weeks and months and years that preceded that given Tuesday and put aside thoughts of what might happen in the days, months, and years following that Tuesday? What if you viewed *that* Tuesday as an opportunity for God to show Himself strong in your life? What if you got up that Tuesday morning and said with the psalmist words like these: "This is the day the LORD has made; [I] will rejoice and be glad in it" (Psalm 118:24 NKJV)? It might very well be the best Tuesday of your life—and one that you will remember for years to come.

The third letter of Stewart's GSAC acronym is *A* for ACCEPT. I can't begin to tell you how important this concept is to a good reaction, in golf and in life. As Stewart put it, "I want to be ready to accept any of my results. I mean *any* result on *any* shot." Why? Because if you don't accept that result, if you refuse to accept it, it's still with you, you're still in turmoil, casting a shadow on your next shot and possibly on your whole round.

As you are aware, this is a prominent theme in the little book you hold in your hands—and it applies to life in Christ just as much as it does to a golf

game. Whatever happens on a particular shot, whether it results in a birdie, an embarrassing bogey, or a hole in one, is history, and you can do nothing about it. What counts, what you can still affect, is the next shot. And this is really the only productive way to live.

Earlier in the book I quoted from Philippians 3:12–14. Here it is again from *The Living Bible*, with my added italics:

> I don't mean to say I am perfect. I haven't learned all I should even yet, but I keep working toward that day when I will finally be all that Christ saved me for and wants me to be.
>
> No, dear brothers, I am still not all I should be, *but I am bringing all my energies to bear on this one thing: Forgetting the past and looking forward to what lies ahead, I strain to reach the end of the race and receive the prize* for which God is calling us up to heaven because of what Christ Jesus did for us.

In a golf tournament you can allow one really terrible shot to haunt you, trouble you, trip you up, spoil the rest of your round, and darken your whole day. In life you can allow regrets, mistakes, sins, and missed opportunities to cast a shadow over a day, a week, a year, or a lifetime. Don't do that! Accept what you have done (or what was done to you); accept that you got off course; accept the help, forgiveness, and grace available in Christ; and then get back in the game! As the apostle Paul wrote, the present time is of the highest importance—it is time to wake up to reality. (Romans 13:11) Who knows what you may accomplish, with God's help, on the very next shot?

The final letter in Stewart's GSAC acronym is *C* for COMMITMENT. In reference to golf Stewart expressed it like this: "I try to commit to what I'm doing before I ever walk into the ball with my pre-shot routine. I already know what I'm going to do, and that the rest of it is up to me and in my control. After that ball is in the air, however, it's no longer in my control, and it's time to move on."

Here's the bottom line: If the full weight of your trust is in the Lord and you're walking with Him in the best way you know how, you can move with optimism and confidence into each day that the Lord gives you.

Some twenty-five hundred years ago, the prophet Jeremiah put this life principle into a graphic word picture:

This is what the Lord says:

> "Cursed is the one who trusts in man,
>   who draws strength from mere flesh
>   and whose heart turns away from the Lord.
> That person will be like a bush in the wastelands;
>   they will not see prosperity when it comes.
> They will dwell in the parched places of the desert,
>   in a salt land where no one lives.
> "But blessed is the one who trusts in the Lord,
>   whose confidence is in him.
> They will be like a tree planted by the water
>   that sends out its roots by the stream.
> It does not fear when the heat comes;
>   its leaves are always green.
> It has no worries in a year of drought
>   and never fails to bear fruit."
>
> JEREMIAH 17:5–8

In other words, if you trust in yourself alone—your skills, your experience, your wisdom, your strength, your personality, your track record, your self-discipline—a day will come when those things will fail you. It may not be tomorrow or the next day, but that day will come. And as

Jeremiah said, you'll find yourself in a wilderness, asking yourself, "How in the world did I get here?"

But if your confidence is in the One who never fails, the One who has promised never to forsake you, you won't fear the dry times or the dark days.

You will have a confidence beyond your own.

CHAPTER 4

Relax: The Priority of Rest

For this game you need, above all things,
to be in a tranquil state of mind.

—HARRY VARDON

Strangely, one of the most talked about moments emerging from the 2010 Ryder Cup competition in Newport, Wales, grew out of Stewart Cink's taking time to eat half a peanut butter sandwich.

One golf writer apparently invested a little time in creating an appropriate headline for the story: "Ryder Cup: Stewart Cink, Powered by Peanut Butter, Pures a Pivotal Putt."[1]

Not to be outdone, AOL News declared, "Stewart Cink Dishes on PB&J Stall." A later story from the same source read: "Despite Peanut Butter, US Finds Itself in Ryder Cup Jam."[2]

Setting that sticky incident aside for a moment, the Ryder Cup competition was a memorable battle from beginning to end. Some in the media called that year's Ryder Cup "one of the most exciting in the 83-year history of the team golf competition,"[3] with the outcome riding on the very last match between Graeme McDowell and Hunter Mahan.

The Europeans went on to win the trophy that Sunday, but no one who watched the competition is likely to forget the amazing 30-foot putt that Stewart Cink made on Saturday at the 17th hole.

And the peanut butter sandwich that preceded it.

The play had been halted that morning after a deluge of rain, but the players had been told to expect to be called back into action that afternoon if the weather cleared. This was partner golf, foursomes, and Stewart had been paired with Matt Kuchar against an Irish duo of Rory McIlroy and Graeme McDowell. Before the rain got too heavy and the officials called a halt to play, the teams had battled to a tie.

Now they were headed down to the 17th hole to finish the match. It was an exciting prospect, but Stewart remembered a certain empty feeling that came over him. He was hungry! He described the scene like this: "They'd just told us that Matt and I were going to go back out for the afternoon round also, and to be prepared when we finished the morning round. My first thought was, *I want something to eat!*"

As Stewart's wife, Lisa—who was in the gallery that day—could attest, her husband didn't like to miss meals. At 6'4" and over 200 pounds, Stewart was a big man who liked to stay "fueled up" when he was competing.

Thankfully, the Ryder Cup staff had thought of that and made provision. "They had some peanut butter sandwiches for the golfers in a cart if we needed something to eat," Stewart recalled. "And I did! So I hustled down to the cart, grabbed a sandwich, and then started back toward the green."

In the meantime, the thirty-year-old McDowell, who went first, hit a magnificent tee shot that rolled to a stop just 6 feet from the pin, leaving his teammate Rory McIlroy with a reasonably easy putt. Predictably, the European fans in the gallery let loose with a roar that shook the ground. American Matt Kuchar's shot gave them something else to cheer about, as it fell considerably short of that mark. Stewart would be looking at a very challenging 30-foot putt.

In the meantime, he was munching down his sandwich. Or trying to.

"There was something about that European peanut butter," he explained. "It was different. I was chewing on that sandwich, but it kept sticking to the roof of my mouth. It took me a little longer than I thought to wolf it down. As it turned out, the announcers on TV were saying that I was deliberately trying to slow-play the Europeans and make them think about their putt. Which was completely false! I was just trying to get my sandwich eaten."

Nevertheless, the assembled media that day reported the incident as a "stall." Stewart, they claimed, was deliberately trying to get into the heads of the Europeans and make them nervous.

One of the writers described it like this: "Cink ate casually. Then he took a nice long drink of water. He licked his lips and began reading his putt. He walked to the left and back to the right. He looked at it from front and back. Players are supposed to have 60 seconds to play their shot, but Cink managed to chew up a little more than three minutes."[4]

Finally, giving up on the sandwich, Stewart handed over the remains to his caddie—who promptly wolfed down the rest of it.

"So I marked the ball," Stewart said, "got ready to putt, and made it! A 30 footer! It was awesome. A huge moment and a huge point in the match. It was just one of those moments where the process worked and the ball went right in the center."

The few Americans in the gallery sent up a cheer, while the Europeans fell silent. McIlroy, with a chance to tie the score again, and (supposedly) unnerved by waiting so long for his putt and the opportunity to tie again, missed his 6-footer.

After the match, and in the days to follow, the press was unwilling to let go of their version of the story: the wily veteran Cink had "schooled" the rookie McIlroy, allowing his young competitor to tighten up—as that 6-foot putt looked longer and longer as the seconds ticked by.

Repeatedly, Stewart tried to put that version to rest with his denials:

> "The peanut butter and jelly were sticking to the roof of my mouth, and I didn't want to hit that putt, being an important putt, with food in my mouth. They kind of got on my case on TV about how I was icing the other guys, but first of all, let's just set the record straight: there is no such thing as icing in golf, because the longer it takes you to hit your shot, you're icing yourself as much as you are icing anybody. So that's ridiculous."

No matter how golf legend and lore record the event, the fact was that Stewart was simply *relaxing* before stepping up to the green to refocus before his shot. He wasn't thinking about McIlroy's putt or the match being tied or the worldwide audience. He was thinking about his stomach rumbling and those peanut butter sandwiches in the refreshment cart.

Relaxing is the fourth *R* of the 4-Rs and is every bit as important as the first three.

Believe it or not, thinking about golf constantly is almost always counterproductive to great golf.

You have to learn to enjoy the journey of the day.

Playing relaxed, even under intense competitive situations, is a process you can learn to control—and even excel in. Remaining in a relaxed state is critical to achieving peak performance, but each person has to develop his or her own formula for staying relaxed between shots.

Once again, here is the key: realize that you don't constantly need to think about golf—even in the middle of a competitive round. You don't have to obsess about your score, your routine, your swing, or your strategy.

You might imagine that such thoughts indicate a "good focus," but they don't. In fact, they will eventually deplete you, wear you down, blur your focus, and end up hurting you instead of helping you. Instead, what you want to do is learn how to focus effectively *at the right time on the right things.* As a general rule, you should only be focusing on golf for about one minute for each shot. This is the approximate amount of time it takes to make a decision, go through your routine, and swing. So in a four-hour round, you may only be focused on golf for seventy, eighty, or ninety minutes, depending on the number of shots played.

Nick Watney thinks it would boil down to even less time than that. "One of the great challenges," he said, "is that you have so much time in between the actual shots. I'll bet if you could magically teleport yourself to the ball after every shot, you could probably finish a round in fifteen minutes. But as it is, you have so much time in between your shots to think about things, good and bad, that it makes it very difficult sometimes to keep your focus."

One golf writer added this thought about all that extra time in a golf match:

What many people do in this spare 3 hours in every round is to get down on themselves mentally. Just watch how many golfers trudge between shots with their heads down and seemingly just staring at the ground a few feet ahead. Many of them are talking to themselves and often what they're saying is not usually fit for publication. Thankfully, they normally keep the voice

inside their heads, but I'm sure you've played the odd round with a playing partner who berates himself loudly during the course of a round—I know I've done that in the, hopefully distant, past and I'm not proud of it.[5]

That's why it's helpful to release your golf focus in between those moments when you stand behind the ball.

You may say to yourself, "Well, if I'm not going to think about golf between shots, then what in the world am I *supposed* to think about?" There are hundreds of different things you can do and think about, all more productive than worrying about your swing or your score. First and foremost, realize that in spite of everything, golf is a *game*, and it is one you choose to play. Golf is not a matter of life and death, and no one is forcing those clubs into your hands. Even professional golfers must realize that in the final analysis,

they're playing a game. Their "work" is to put in the long hours of practice early in the week and before and after rounds. From Thursday to Sunday, this is their time to "show off," have fun, and enjoy the thrill of competition.

Think of Stewart Cink. Before one of the biggest golf shots of his whole career, he went looking for the refreshment cart to check out the sandwiches! While the gallery and media were oohing and aahing over McDowell's amazing tee shot, Stewart was strolling to the green trying to swallow a mouthful of peanut butter. When he arrived, he went right into his refocus, then routine, and then he drained a 30-foot putt.

What do you think about between shots? If you're not a professional, be glad you're not "at work"! Enjoy the walk or the ride in a cart. Look at the trees and the roll of the terrain. Notice how the sun shimmers on the water in the ponds or creeks. If the course has wildlife, take time to enjoy the ducks or geese, or count the turtles sitting on a log in the pond. If you like architecture, study the houses around the course. Imagine funny shapes in the clouds overhead like you did when you were a kid. Think about a good movie you saw or a book you'd like to read. Enjoy these opportunities to focus on something besides golf and your round. *Above all else, learn to enjoy the journey of the day.*

As you are well aware, at some point in every round (or in every day of life, for that matter) something will surely happen to challenge your peace of mind and your enjoyment of the journey. It may be a missed putt or a drive out of bounds. Or it may be a slow group ahead of you who won't let you play through. How you react to this situation will largely determine how well you are able to continue playing.

If you find yourself angry or depressed over your play or some other circumstance on the course, you may have to use the emotion zone to recompose yourself (remembering to keep that zone very small and limited). Or you may have to walk away from the situation for a moment or two and talk to yourself about how you aren't going to allow *anything* to distract you from making the most of your day. It may mean, for instance, walking away from the tee box for a while instead of standing there waiting to play.

Shift your focus from the hole and the target to something entirely different. Tell a joke if you feel like it. Just don't stand there and stress about the waiting you have to do, because in many situations, there isn't a thing you can do about it. When it's time to play, play. Until then focus on something else.

Some players on the tour, notably Phil Mickelson and Boo Weekley, relax by talking with their playing partners or their caddies, or even chatting with people in the gallery in the course of a round. Conversely, pros like Tiger Woods or Retief Goosen almost never interact with the crowd during a round. Your style may be like Phil or Tiger or somewhere in between. If you're not a talker, don't force it. Be yourself in a way that you are most comfortable. If you prefer not to talk and a playing partner talks nonstop, don't walk close to him—or let him drive the cart and you walk. Remember, this is your relaxation journey, so don't let others take you out of your mode.

Relaxing on the golf course, especially in an intense competitive situation, is one of the great challenges of the game. Nevertheless, it's a challenge that you can learn to control and excel in. Once you do, and only once you do, will you achieve lower scores and have more fun at the same time. Remember, the journey will have some twists and turns and undoubtedly a few bumps. Welcome to golf! Welcome to life! The key is reacting to those unexpected intrusions and circumstances with composure.

Even so, relaxing isn't always easy, even for the pros. Jonathan Byrd has said that "overthinking" and "wanting to be in control" are two of his biggest struggles in any given round. He has also admitted that it carries over into even deeper areas of his life. "I'm a perfectionist," he said, "and I feel like I have to make everything line up all the time. But God is the One who is in control. So sometimes, for me, it's just a matter of letting go."

LIFE APPLICATION

FINDING CONTENTMENT WITH WHATEVER LIFE BRINGS

Of all the shots and putts I've discussed with my players over the years, there's one we've never spoken about that impresses me the most. In 2001, on the 72nd hole of the second major that year, the US Open, Stewart Cink missed an 18-inch putt that would have put him in a play-off for the title. We're talking 18 *inches* here—not 18 feet.

You might think it strange that it was never part of our dialogue since we started working together in 2009. But I don't find it strange at all.

It's not because it's too hard to talk about. It's not because Stewart doesn't want to go there because it's too painful.

No, it's because Stewart has moved on. He has accepted what happened in 2001, and he is content with it. He makes no effort to go back and relive that thin little slice of his life. Why? Because he knows God has a plan for him, and that his job is to glorify God and accept the results. He has confidence in God's plan. And if you have confidence in God's plan, you will live life forward, not backward.

"Golf tests you every day in a hundred ways," said Stewart. "It pokes and prods at you to find out what you're made of. It's the same in our walk with Christ. We're constantly being tested—sometimes in painful ways, and sometimes in very subtle ways. We always have to be ready to respond. In both golf and the Christian life, you never know on a given day what's going to come at you."

In other words, you persevere. You glorify. You accept. You don't give up on your routine. You don't abandon your process. And you never write off a day before it's over.

If something negative happens in your day, if you encounter a disappointment or a setback, you don't let it cast a shadow over the rest of your day. A day is hanging in the balance, and that is no small thing. After all, we are only given so many days.

I have a friend who lost his wife to cancer while she was still in her forties. Looking back, my friend can remember so many days that were marred by his own irritation, impatience, or melancholy over incidents he can't even remember now. He wishes he could have some of those days back. Each one was precious, though that realization didn't penetrate his mind-set at the time.

The fact is, we don't get second chances on days gone by. But unless we have already passed on, we do have the gift and the wonder of another twenty-four hours to live a better way and make better choices.

And if we choose, we can practice contentment with what God has given us. No, it isn't always easy. But there is help—amazing, indescribable help. Listen to the words of Jesus in *The Message* translation of Matthew 11:28–30:

Are you tired? Worn out? Burned out on religion? Come to me. Get away with me and you'll recover your life. I'll show you how to take a real rest. Walk with me and work with me—watch how I do it. Learn the unforced rhythms of grace. I won't lay anything heavy or ill-fitting on you. Keep company with me and you'll learn to live freely and lightly.

Don't you love that? Freely. Lightly. Unforced. At rest. Content.

If you can't live freely, if you can't live without worrying and stressing all the time, if you can't find contentment with what God has provided you, then what does that say?

It may say that your confidence is in the wrong place. Or more specifically, the wrong person.

If you can't relax in golf, it's because you don't trust your own process. If you can't relax in life, there's a good chance you don't trust God's plans for you.

In life, make the most of every day, wherever you are, whatever your circumstances. Trust Him. Link up with Jesus, and He will show you how. When you're playing partners with the One who created the universe, it doesn't matter how you hit your tee shot. Just get in the cart with Him and ride.

If you can't relax in golf, it's because you don't trust your own process. If you can't relax in life, there's a good chance you don't trust God's plans for you.

CONCLUSION

Invite the Challenge

Golf is the closest game to the game we call
life. You get bad breaks from good shots;
you get good breaks from bad shots—but
you have to play the ball where it lies.

—BOBBY JONES

T he morning before the final round of the Masters at Augusta
in 2007, Zach Johnson and I sat down for a little talk. He was
in a three-way tie for fourth place, with Tiger Woods, Justin
Rose, and Stuart Appleby ahead of him. He had played well and stayed
with his game, but no one really expected him to contend for the title.
Everybody knew Augusta was a "big hitters' course," and Zach was
never known for that. Was he serious about following a conservative
strategy of trying to make birdies rather than eagles—not even trying
to hit the 5-par holes in 2? And anyway, how could he hope to match up
with Tiger Woods? Hadn't Tiger already won going away at the Buick
Invitational and Doral?

I knew this was no time for teaching new material or for loading him up
with a dozen things to remember. He was already trusting his routine and
playing his own game. So I made a few quick points and left it at that.

First, I told him that there was no way either of us could foretell how the day would unfold. To waste any time and energy wondering and speculating about the final results was just that—wasted time.

Zach nodded. He'd done very well keeping such results—and all that went with them—out of the forefront of his thoughts. He'd been playing one hole at a time, and I was proud of him for it.

Second, I told him that what he had been doing was working—and there was no reason to think it would stop working just because he was heading into the final day. He simply needed to stick with his plan. To trust and go.

Zach had heard it all before, of course. But sometimes when you find yourself in a place of great pressure, it's good to hear familiar counsel again and affirm its truth.

Finally, I gave him three simple points to carry him through the biggest golfing day of his life to that point.

"First, Zach, invite the challenge of every shot. Second, keep playing the golf course. And third, believe in your routine, believe in your preparation, and believe in yourself."

Zach did those things and later that day walked right into the history books.

Most people can handle a challenge.

Many people can overcome a challenge.

But it takes a special person to *invite* a challenge.

In golf (and in life), however, this is what you must do. You have to love the cold, the rain, and the wind. You have to embrace the bad breaks, the unfortunate bounces, the sand traps, and those strange times when the ball rolls into the hole and rolls right back out again. You have to savor wearing extra clothes and the changing conditions.

And you can't just endure it; you have to *relish* it.

Nothing truly worthwhile comes easy. And when the challenge comes—whatever it is and wherever it comes from—you have to meet it head on, welcome it, invite it into your life, and overcome it.

One of the golf professionals I've had the privilege to work with who has embraced this concept most fully is Davis Love III—who in turn learned it from two of his heroes: his dad, Davis Love Jr., and the legendary Tom Watson.

In the final round of The Players Championship 2003 (sometimes known as The Players), Davis shot a 64 in dreadful weather conditions to win the tournament. The Players, which takes place in Sawgrass, Florida, is sometimes referred to as the "fifth major" but doesn't have official major status. Even so, the winner's share of the purse is the highest prize of any tournament in golf and wins him more points toward his official world golf ranking than any event outside of the majors.

So it's a big deal.

And wouldn't you know it, the final round that year was played on a day of driving rain and gusting wind. It was just plain cold, something you don't usually associate with springtime in Florida.

But when Davis Love III pulled back the curtains of his hotel room on Sunday morning to see wind-whipped rain streaming down the glass, he smiled.

"When the conditions are bad," Davis told me, "I always feel like a good ball striker is going to be ahead. I learned that from Tom Watson. I

> When the challenge comes—whatever
> it is and wherever it comes from—you
> have to meet it head on, welcome it, invite
> it into your life, and overcome it.

learned to love the fact that most guys are not going to be happy with bad weather and the conditions on the course. They'll be complaining to one another. They'll say, 'It's too windy. It's too cold. It's too wet. It's just too hard. I'm not comfortable. I hate this.'"

When Davis hears comments like those on the practice tee or in the locker room, he feels good all over.

"I always felt like I had an advantage at those times if I kept a good attitude. My dad always played well when the weather was bad or the greens were bad, because he always had a brighter outlook and a more positive attitude. And Tom Watson? The worse the weather got, the cockier he became."

Apparently, when the golf conditions became nasty, Tom Watson was able to bring an even tighter focus to his extraordinary game. He once said, "Confidence in golf means being able to concentrate on the problem at hand with no outside interference."[1]

Watson would have no doubt applauded Davis's mind-set as he headed into that stormy, blustery morning at the Players. "I was playing with Freddy Couples on that Sunday," he said, "which was a good pairing. And I just went out with the attitude, *This is my opportunity to take advantage of my talent and my attitude. I've already beaten half the guys in the tournament, because they're angry and upset, and I'm happy.*"

Davis made a couple of putts on the first few holes, and that put him right into the groove. While the other players were griping and shivering, Davis was driving the ball hard and nailing his putts.

"I was just playing my own game," he said, "and not worrying about the weather. Really, I hardly even noticed that the weather was bad. When things cleared up later in the round, I still had my rain jacket on."

When someone commented on the fact that Davis was still playing in his jacket, Fred Couples laughed and basically told them to leave his partner alone. He said, "Davis would rather lose his driver than his rain jacket! He doesn't want to take it off. He always plays good in his rain jacket."[2]

"Freddy was right," Davis said. "I'm happy in my rain jacket. I'm happy in the bad weather. I remember a tournament in Greensboro back in 1992 when the weather was absolutely terrible. I shot a 62 and was 10 under par when nobody else shot below a 68."

It had been cold, wet, miserable, and windy, and Davis loved every minute of it.

Time and again, Davis has credited his favorite champion, Tom Watson. When the wind started blowing and the rain started coming down, he recalled how Watson would look up with a smile and say, "Hey, this is the day for me!" And it wasn't irony. He meant it!

An Associated Press reporter described Davis's triumph at the Players with these words:

> "The guys playing alongside and behind him called it one of the greatest rounds they had ever seen. And this time they weren't talking about Tiger Woods. Davis Love III hit all the shots and made all the crucial putts Sunday in The Players Championship, closing with an 8-under 64 in cold, blustery conditions for a victory he ranks among his best."[3]

Fred Couples, Davis's playing partner, friend, and a twenty-three-year member of the PGA tour at that time, said, "It's the best round of golf I've ever seen played." John "Cubby" Burke, Davis's caddie on that day and a seventeen-year tour veteran himself, was also in awe. "One of the best rounds I've ever watched in my life," he said.[4]

When Saturday's play ended, Davis was two strokes behind.

And then on Sunday morning he woke up, saw the rain, watched the slender pine trees bending in the wind, and suddenly felt very, very good.

With the wind tugging at his blue rain jacket and threatening to pull the cap off his head, he shocked his competitors and the gallery with five straight birdies, and it was off to the races from there. By the time the tournament wrapped up that afternoon, Davis had matched the best closing round in the thirty-year history of the Players Championship and had claimed the richest prize on the PGA tour.

The Associated Press writer marveled at my friend's calm play in the face of adversity: "Even into the crosswinds, the most challenging in golf, Love blasted his drives down the middle of the fairway, and stuck his approach shots close to the hole.

'You can't do that for 18 holes, and he did it," Couples said. "In these conditions, he did not miss a shot.'"[5]

Davis, who loves to talk about some of the golf legends of years gone by, remembered his dad telling a story about Gary Player and what a positive player he was.

"He would say to Dad, 'Oh, Davis, I *love* the greens this week! I love the bent grass greens. They're the finest greens ever.' And then the next week

when they would be playing on Bermuda grass, Player would exult, 'Oh, aren't these Bermuda greens great, Davis? These are my favorite.'

"Dad would remind him, 'You liked the bent grass greens last week!'

"The thing is, you just talk yourself into a positive attitude about whatever the situation is. Gary Player once said, 'We create success or failure on the course primarily by our thoughts.'" Davis does this by looking for the positive, picking it out and focusing on it, even if there are negative things swirling all around. He admits, however, that this attitude didn't come naturally to him. "I learned it," he told me, "from all the time I've spent with mental golf coaches like you and Dr. Bob Rotella. You make your own attitude. I remember my dad saying to me, 'Don't let your golf game determine your attitude; let your attitude determine your golf game.'"

Davis reminds me how I would always tell him, "Just because it's cold and windy doesn't mean you don't get into your routine."

"That day at the Players," he said, "I'd determined to play my own game and follow my routine. And the next thing I knew, every putt was going in. What I've learned from you, Dr. Mo, is that there is a way to practice that, even if you're not particularly good at it."

Part of what Davis refers to here is the method I use for teaching players how to develop a **positive**, **resilient mind-set**.

Here's how it breaks down.

When you're **positive**, you expect good things to happen. You believe that future shots and rounds will be progressively better.

This doesn't mean you do your best imitation of Pollyanna or act like the little boy who happily dug through a room filled with horse manure, saying, "I know there must be a pony in here somewhere!" No, it doesn't mean you ignore the realities around you or never get upset on the golf course. It simply means that you have made a firm choice to view past, present, and future events in a way that will be helpful to your future success.

When you're **resilient**, it means you maintain an unchanging thought process regardless of your circumstances or the events of any given day. In other words, how you *think* doesn't change based on how you might be playing. If you're playing inspired golf—at the top of your game—your thought processes don't change. If you're playing poorly—even having a career bad day—your thought processes don't change. *You let your thinking dictate your play, not your play dictate your thinking.*

If you combine positive and resilient thinking, you end up with an expectation that good things are going to happen regardless of how you are currently playing. If you're playing poorly, things will get better. If you're playing great, you can play even better than that—and consistently so—over time.

What you develop, as a result of such expectations, is a positive, resilient **mind-set**—essentially a broad, all-encompassing way of thinking about and viewing your game.

Your mind-set is who you are. Your mind-set personifies your core being. Your mind-set will end up determining how you play the game.

In general, most everyone has a good attitude on the first tee. They're laughing, having fun, and looking forward to the round. A good attitude is easy . . . *then*. A positive, resilient mind-set, however, enables you to hold on to a hopeful outlook whether you start birdie, birdie or even bogey, double. Maintaining a positive, resilient mind-set is much more difficult than "having a good attitude." It is also a *must* if you want to consistently improve your game.

It's one thing to simply understand a productive mind-set; it is another to put it into action. Just knowing the 4-Rs won't automatically make them part of your game. *More than anything else, a mind-set takes preparation. And no matter what mind-set you choose, you have the best chance to maintain that mind-set on the course if you have repeatedly thought about it prior to and during the game.*

The best mind-set in the world is no good if you wait until you arrive at the course to come up with it.

I have found the best way for players to truly ingrain such a mind-set into their game is to encourage them to take ten-minute walks before a competitive round and concentrate on how they want to be on the course. More specifically, I want them to talk to themselves about the mind-set they will maintain and visualize what actions accompany that mind-set on the course.

For example, a player who wants to really ingrain the 4-Rs mind-set into his game could take ten-minute walks each day for three to four days prior

to his event. During these walks he would talk to himself about consistently going through his routines, about how he will relax between shots, and how he will let himself trust and simply react to the target. He might also visualize himself going through his routine and hitting great shots and great putts, walking down the fairway very relaxed, and hitting shots fully trusting and reacting as opposed to thinking and trying.

The best mind-set in the world is no good if you wait until you arrive at the course to come up with it.

Stewart Cink has learned to relish the challenge too. "Each hole presents you with a new challenge. Every shot, really. Golf is such a great game because it has so many variables. There are infinite possibilities in the way you can be presented with the game."

So it is in our lives.

The Bible is a book about many things, but one of the great themes running from cover to cover is men and women rising to the challenges in life through faith in God. When the test comes, when the difficulty arises, when the obstacle looms in front of you, don't shy away from the challenge. With God's help, *step into it.*

One of the most familiar stories in the Bible tells how David, a young Jewish shepherd boy, unexpectedly found himself in battle facing a freakish, nine-foot Philistine warrior named Goliath. You've no doubt heard the story somewhere. But what I personally love most about the account is how David approached the fight. The Bible tells us that this teenager, armed only with a sling and a few smooth stones from the brook, "ran quickly toward the battle line to meet him" (1 Samuel 17:48).

Moments later David was standing over the fallen giant, praising God for a great victory.

He ran to the battle line. Nothing illustrates inviting the challenge better than that.

Would I have run toward that battle line? I can't honestly say, but I hope I would have. I can think of a few times when I have—and a number of other occasions when I haven't. It would have been easy for David, small as he was, to play keep-away from Goliath, dodging from tree to tree, twisting, turning, or darting this way and that like an excited terrier. But that's not what David did. Instead, he faced his great enemy, calculated the odds, and ran straight into battle, crying out, "You come against me with sword and spear and javelin, but I come against you in the name of the LORD Almighty, the God of the armies of Israel, whom you have defied. This day the LORD will deliver you into my hands, and I'll strike you down and cut off your head" (1 Samuel 17:45–46).

And that's exactly what he did.

I'm reminded of these words from pastor and author Dr. Charles Swindoll:

> The longer I live, the more I realize the impact of attitude on life. Attitude, to me, is more important than facts. It is more important than the past, than education, than money, than circumstances, than failures, than successes, than what other people think or say or do. It is more important than appearance, giftedness, or skill. It will make or break a company . . . a church . . . a home. The remarkable thing is we have a choice every day regarding the attitude we will embrace that day. We cannot change our past . . . we cannot change the fact that people will act in a certain way. We cannot change the inevitable. The only thing we can do is play on the one string we have, and this is our attitude. . . . I am convinced that life is 10 percent what happens to me, and 90 percent how I react to it.[6]

The first place I remember seeing that quote was taped to the mirror in my parents' bathroom. So you might say that God began teaching me this concept at an early age—even though I didn't know what it meant at the time.

It inspires me to think about how Davis Love III walked into that round of golf at The Players Championship, with the storm all around him, a great challenge before him, and his fellow players grousing about the conditions and cursing their luck. A day of great adversity became a day of unparalleled opportunity. The very circumstances that defeated many others became a tool to push him to one of the greatest victories of his life.

It sounds strange, but sometimes setbacks in a golf tournament can actually help to settle a player down and give him or her more focus. We can see that this is true by going back to Zach Johnson's Sunday round at the Masters. He was in the third group, just two shots back, and in a position to make a move. So what did he achieve on the first hole that morning?

A bogey.

"It settled me down," Zach recalled.

"Just that quickly I found myself three shots back, and the leaders hadn't even teed off yet. The idea of winning, which had seemed so impossible, now seemed that much more impossible. *But it also made it that much more fun to try!* When I came away with a bogey, it was like, 'Well, at least I got *that* out of the way.' Then I had a little talk with myself, and said, 'Zach, you're not supposed to win this anyway, so just go play!' I birdied the next two holes, started to look at the scoreboard, and then asked myself, 'Why are you even doing that?' I think I made another bogey on the front nine, but when I made the turn for the final nine, I really felt peace about the day. It was Easter Sunday, and I planned on enjoying it. Arriving at 18, I felt settled. It felt like I was teeing off on the 36th hole of the tournament rather than the final hole of the Masters."

And as it turned out, Zach made par on the final hole, won the tournament, and had an Easter Sunday he would remember for the rest of his life.

But it doesn't always work out that way, does it? There will be those times when you aren't able to overcome the odds, and your adversities bring you to a defeat rather than a surprise triumph. Even in those times, God can still work through your life in more ways than you realize.

"Success," says Zach Johnson, "isn't always on the scorecard. Winning isn't always based on numbers or stats or hoisting up a trophy with everyone cheering for you. Yes, it's a great opportunity when a Christian athlete can give thanks to God and profess his faith after winning a tournament. But what you don't see are the guys who give glory to God even when they lose. Nobody has a camera in your face when you finish 45th in a tournament. But the guys I've looked up to, the guys who have inspired me, are the guys who sign their scorecards—whether on Thursday or Sunday, whether they win or lose—and still are able to give glory to God. That, to me, is a successful day. That is winning.

"You may not even have to say anything. It may just be the way you walk, the way you hold your shoulders. There is no set way to glorify the Lord when you're not winning—but that doesn't mean you won't have an opportunity to do so. Sometimes, even when you aren't successful, you'll hear another golfer say, 'I like how you play the game. You always seem to have a peace about you no matter what your scorecard says or what you shot that day.' That's the kind of stuff you want to hear.

"I hope that's true of me. I hope I'm still living my faith even when I'm not winning. You might not see the results on TV, but you can be sure that someone somewhere is watching."

Winning at golf is one of life's great privileges and pleasures.
But it doesn't hold a candle to winning at life.

My Story and My Commitment

Nobody ever promised you life would be fair. To change your life, you have to change the way you think.

HARVEY PENICK

You may have noticed me on a putting green somewhere or seen me on TV and wondered, *How did that guy get into this sports psychology stuff?* It all began when I was seventeen years old, a junior in high school, and I was watching a basketball program on TV late one night. There was a guy who worked with the Utah Jazz basketball team, and they said he was a sports psychologist. He was just hanging out with the team, spending time in the gym, and talking to the players. He sat on the bench during games and rode around with the team on a private plane.

I thought to myself, *They're paying this guy to do that? I've got to look into this!*

Not long after that I'd made up my mind—that is what I wanted to do with my life. That's the direction I wanted to go. So before I ever even

Left to right trophies from the four major championships: The Open Championship, The Masters, The PGA, and The US Open. Players have won three of these four trophies while working with Dr. Pickens.

enrolled in college, I knew that I would have to go on to graduate school and that it would be a long road.

At that point in my life, I was big into collecting quotes. One of my favorites was from an Indian Chief in the 1700s named Tecumseh, who said, "From my tribe I take nothing. I am the maker of my own fortune."[1]

I liked the sound of that very much. I remember telling myself, "That's how I'm going to live. That's the path I'm going to follow. I'll work hard, I'll study hard, and I'll make my own fortune." I knew that I would put in the time and effort and sacrifice to reach my goals, and ultimately become successful.

So that's what I did. I went to Clemson, did well academically, then went on to graduate school at the University of Virginia, graduating in 1995 with a PhD in sports psychology.

Everything was going along according to plan. After graduate school and a year-long internship in Charlotte, North Carolina, we (my wife, Suzanne, and toddler daughter, Sellers) moved to Columbia, South Carolina, and soon bought our first house. From all outward appearances, it looked like I was achieving the outcomes I had set for myself since high school and was doing so with success.

Chief Tecumseh would be proud, wouldn't he?

While we lived in Columbia, we started attending church regularly. At that time I really didn't grasp what they were talking about from Sunday to Sunday or what it had to do with me. After all, my life was on course—on the very trajectory I had set out for myself. Church was something we did socially, because in our part of the country, that's what many respectable people did.

But then something strange began to happen at that church.

For some reason, I started listening. Something had changed, or maybe I began to change. I'm really not sure which happened first. The teaching was different somehow. We had some new teachers in our young adult Sunday school class who rocked me back on my heels a little. They were making me

> When people say they receive Christ and their thinking changes, they're telling the truth.

think about life on a whole different level than I was used to. In what seemed to me a short amount of time, church became something more than socializing, meeting and greeting, seeing and being seen. I started hanging out with some guys who were part of an informal Bible study. These were men who obviously took the Bible and their relationship with God more seriously than I'd been accustomed to doing. Without intending to make any changes in my life at all, I felt myself being drawn in.

My daughter, Sellers, was seven at the time, and Suzanne and I took her into the hospital one morning for what we thought would be a routine tonsillectomy. But as it turned out, it wasn't routine at all. Far from it. As Sellers was coming out of surgery, she developed pulmonary edema—a sometimes fatal condition where fluid begins to fill the lungs. In fact, Sellers's lungs collapsed, and she was rushed to ICU at Palmetto Richland Memorial Hospital, where she spent the next four days.

The first couple of days in ICU were very touch and go. We thought we might lose our little girl. On the third day, early that morning, I was down in the hospital cafeteria with one of my new friends from the men's Bible study. He prayed with me, and that day I gave my life to Jesus Christ.

In God's grace, our little girl recovered, and our family has expanded to four dear children. But my life had been turned on its head. When people say they receive Christ and their thinking changes, they're telling the truth. It was suddenly as though I was able to look at my life from a completely new perspective. I'd assumed that all the good things that had come to me through

the years were of my own making. But in an instant I realized, "Mo, you don't make *anything*. Nothing has come to you in life except through Him." What I had assumed were trophies in my life—rewarding me for all my diligence, determination, and hard work—weren't trophies at all. They were amazingly kind and generous blessings from the hand of a good and loving God.

From there, I got more and more involved in church and in the men's ministry, and I started learning what having a "relationship" with Christ really meant. We moved to southeast Georgia, and I got hooked up with some strong Christian men in our new church.

I have my office at the beautiful Sea Island Golf Learning Center in St. Simons Island, Georgia. And I hadn't worked there very long before I started taking a walk around part of the course early in the morning. On those walks

I began talking to God, just thanking Him for all of His blessings. For how He came to earth for me. Died for me. Rose again for me. For how He had forgiven me and helped me. For the wonderful wife and family He'd given me.

These were sincere expressions of gratitude from my heart, but it never occurred to me at that time that all of those blessings ended with the word *me*. My focus was still on me, what I now possessed and my blessings.

Jesus told a story in Matthew 13:1–23 about a farmer who scattered seed in an area where thorns came up and choked the plants, making them unfruitful. Jesus used the example to speak of the kind of person whose relationship with God gets squeezed out by the worries and anxieties and preoccupations of everyday life. That's a good picture of me sometimes. I know that deep down I want to follow God and live for God, but that desire gets choked out by the worries and concerns of *my* everyday life.

Early last year, however, at a church men's retreat, I was confronted with a concept from the Bible that has given me more perspective than ever. It's based on Galatians 2:20. In that passage, the apostle Paul said: "I have been crucified with Christ and I no longer live, but Christ lives in me. The life I now live in the body, I live by faith in the Son of God, who loved me and gave himself for me." *I no longer live, but Christ lives in me.*

I told the guys in my small group at that study that whether I'd intended it or not, whether I was even aware of it or not, I'd been living my life based on three words: *Focus on me.* Even if I was thinking about the blessings in my life, they were *my* blessings—and the focus was still on *me*. So I've really been trying to change from a *focus on me*—the three words—to those other nine words: *I no longer live, but Christ lives in me.*

When I said this, Skip, one of my new friends and a mathmetician of sorts, said, "Mo, the only way you can get from three to nine is through a Higher Power." Skip is right. I need a strength beyond my own to live this way.

The beauty of the new perspective that I received that weekend was that by *my*self, through *my* own actions, with *my* thoughts guiding me, there is no way I can glorify God one moment at a time and become more Christlike. The only way this can happen is by letting the Holy Spirit within me take over. I have to let Him guide me through the process He has given me. It works like this: He leads, and I follow. He lives in me, and I die to my old self-centered ways. The process isn't complicated, but it will take a lifetime to achieve.

You don't have to remind me that I have the best job in the world. I get to play golf every day, hang out with some remarkable players, and teach skills that I know, beyond a shadow of a doubt, will improve anyone's golf game. The very thought of it makes me smile.

But if any of the words in this book prompt you to seek a closer relationship with Jesus Christ, the Creator of all things and the Lord of life, that "win" is bigger than any of the victories my players could ever achieve. If you know Jesus as your Savior and Lord, then for sure, I'll see you in eternity, somewhere on the back nine.

Everyone knows there's golf in heaven.

As you walk down the fairway of life you must smell the roses, for you only get to play one round.

BEN HOGAN

A Final Word

I t's one thing to daydream about a better golf game, but it's another thing entirely to put together a structured plan that moves you toward actual, tangible, measurable goals. The same can be said about your relationship with God. If a closer relationship with Him is something you truly desire, then it is important to keep a few goals in mind as you go through each day.

What follows are four life applications taken from the pages of this book. I suggest that you write them on a card and put them in a place where you will see them daily—on your computer or your mirror or the refrigerator door. You might want to restate them in your own words, or add your own. However you decide, find a process that works for you.

Application #1: A fresh commitment to seek the Lord every day.

Application #2: A consistent walk along the right path.

Application #3: A confident acceptance of God's plan for my life.

Application #4: A settled contentment with whatever life brings to my doorstep.

Golf and life are parallel partners. Each one is a process that never finds perfection. The journey is filled with great joy when you learn to live the process one day at a time.

About the Author

D r. Morris Pickens (or Dr. Mo, as his students call him), is the Sports Psychologist and Performance Specialist at the Sea Island Golf Learning Center. He has been a coach to some of the best golfers in the world. His students have won over 200 amateur titles, 30 professional tournaments, three major golf championships, and one NCAA Championship. He lives in St. Simons Island, Georgia, with his wife and four children.

Notes

INTRODUCTION: ONE SHOT AT A TIME

1. Damon Hack, "Zach Johnson Wins the Masters," *New York Times*, April 8, 2007, http://www.nytimes.com/2007/04/09/sports/09iht-web-0409masters.5195529.html?_r=0.
2. Interview with the collaborator. All subsequent quotes are taken from personal interviews with the collaborators unless otherwise noted.
3. Goodreads, http://www.goodreads.com/quotes/12747-wherever-you-are-be-*all*-there-live-to-the-hilt.

CHAPTER 1. REFOCUS: REGAINING YOUR DIRECTION

1. "Lee Trevino," Golf Today, http://www.golftoday.co.uk/noticeboard/quotes/trevino.html.
2. Mark Orlovac, "Cink Dashes Watson's Open Dreams," BBC Sport/Golf, July 19, 2009, http://news.bbc.co.uk/sport2/hi/golf/8158269.stm.
3. "The Open Championship," Golf Today, http://www.golftoday.co.uk/noticeboard/quotes/open_championship.html#b1YyBVpIfYLjpKcY.99.
4. "Toughest 18 Holes in Golf," Golf.com, http://www.golf.com/photos/hardest-18-holes-golf/doral.

CHAPTER 2. ROUTINE: MAXIMIZE YOUR PREPARATION

1. http://www.youtube.com/watch?v=F5CvsG7olm0
2. http://sports.espn.go.com/golf/news/story?id=5724455

CHAPTER 3. REACT: TRUST AND GO

1. Liz Bergren, "The Masters Mystique," Golf Digest.com, April 2012, http://www.golfdigest.com/golf-tours-news/golf-masters/2012-04/photos-quotes-on-the-masters#slide=1.
2. Associated Press, "Zach Johnson Wins Masters Golf Tournament," FoxNews.com, April 8, 2007, http://www.foxnews.com/story/2007/04/08/zach-johnson-wins-masters-golf-tournament/.
3. "Zach Johnson," https://en.wikipedia.org/wiki/Zach_Johnson#cite_note-2.
4. Associated Press, "Zach Wins John Deere," ESPN.com, July 15, 2012, http://espn.go.com/golf/story/_/id/8169044/zach-johnson-tops-troy-matteson-playoff-win-john-deere-classic.
5. Seven Oaks Golf, Quotes, http://www.sevenoaksgolf.com/golf-course/course-information/golf-quotes.

CHAPTER 4. RELAX: THE PRIORITY OF REST

1. "Ryder Cup: Stewart Cink, Powered by Peanut Butter, Pures a Pivotal Putt," Nuther Duffer, October 2, 2010, http://www.nutherduffer.com/2010/10/ryder-cup-stewart-cink-powered-by.html.

2. "Stewart Cink Dishes on PB&J Stall," AOL News, November 10, 2010, http://www.aolnews.com/2010/11/10/stewart-cink-dishes-on-pbandj-stall/.

3. "How the Ryder Cup Was Won," CNN.com, October 4, 2010, http://edition.cnn.com/2010/SPORT/golf/10/04/ryder.cup.in.pictures/index.html.

4. "Stewart Cink Dishes on PB&J Stall," AOL News, November 10, 2010, http://www.aolnews.com/2010/11/10/stewart-cink-dishes-on-pbandj-stall/.

5. Andrew Fogg, "How to Improve Your Mental Golf Approach between Shots with Golf Psychology," http://www.golf-hypnotist.com/how-to-improve-your-mental-golf-approach-between-shots-with-golf-psychology/.

CONCLUSION: INVITE THE CHALLENGE

1. "Tom Watson Quotes," Brainy Quote, http://www.brainyquote.com/quotes/authors/t/tom_watson.html#zKGZCCkvdG6mxm78.99.

2. Associated Press, "Love's 64 Untouchable at Sawgrass," ESPN.com, August 2, 2003, http://sports.espn.go.com/golf/playerschamp/story?id=1531491.

3. Ivan Maisel, "A Love Like No Other," ESPN.com, August 2, 2003, http://sports.espn.go.com/golf/playerschamp/story?id=1531584.

4. AP, "Love's 64 Untouchable at Sawgrass."

5. Dr. Charles R. Swindoll; http://www.selfhelpdaily.com/quote-about-attitude/

AFTERWORD: MY STORY AND MY COMMITMENT

1. "Tecumseh," Brainy Quote, www.brainyquote.com/quotes/quotes/t/tecumseh405067.html.